# *Because He's Worthy*

## Offering Excellent Worship Through Understanding the Scriptures and Practical Music Theory

## Mark Medley

For more information call (865) 521-8000
or write to: Mark Medley, c/o Trinity Chapel, 5830 Haynes Sterchi Rd., Knoxville, TN 37912
Website: www.trinitychapel.com ¥ Email: medleymail@mindspring.com

Copyright 2001 Mark Medley. All Rights Reserved.

# Contents

## Section One – A Biblical Foundation

| | |
|---|---|
| Preface | 5 |
| What is Worship? | 9 |
| What Jesus Taught about Worship | 15 |
| What Happens when We Worship | 23 |
| Seven Spirits of a Worshiper | 31 |
| Levitical Worship: Set Apart for His Service | 43 |
| Worship in the Life of David: A Secret Life with God | 47 |
| The Tabernacle of David, The Tabernacle of God | 53 |
| Priming Your Praise Pump | 59 |
| Worship and the Heart | 63 |
| Our Worship Team Vision | 65 |
| Why We Worship the Way We Do | 67 |
| Definitions | 71 |
| A Brief Look at Church History and Musical Styles | 73 |
| Study Questions | 77 |

## Section Two – Music Theory Applied to Worship

| | |
|---|---|
| Understanding Music Theory | 83 |
| Rhythm | 84 |
| Pitch | 87 |
| Notes of the Grand Staff | 88 |
| Intervals | 89 |
| Major Scale Construction | 90 |
| Key Signatures | 93 |
| Circle of Fifths | 94 |
| Triads and Seventh Chords | 95 |
| Inversions | 96 |
| Diatonic Harmony (Chords within a Key) | 97 |
| Voicing Diatonic Triads and Seventh Chords | 98 |
| How to Learn a Song Quickly | 100 |

| | |
|---|---|
| Functional Harmony | 103 |
| Transposing | 104 |
| Transposition Table for All Keys | 105 |
| Embellishing a Chord Progression | 106 |
| Rhythmic Accompaniment | 108 |
| Dynamic Markings and Musical Symbols | 111 |
| Minor Scales | 112 |
| Other Scales | 113 |
| Possible Chord Progressions for Open Worship | 114 |
| Improvisation | 117 |
| Things to Think about When Approaching a Song | 119 |
| Working with the Team | 121 |
| Practical Issues – Some Ideas that Might Help | 125 |
|     Choosing Band Members | |
|     Running a Practice | |
|     Making a Song List | |
|     Working with Singers | |
|     Incorporating the Choir | |
| The Rhythm Section | 133 |
|     Drums | |
|     Bass | |
|     Rhythm Guitar | |
|     Piano/Keyboard | |
|     Percussion | |
|     Wind and Brass Instruments | |
|     Getting Better | |
| Practical Tips for Prophetic Worship | 141 |
| The Pastor/Worship Leader Relationship | 145 |
| Worship and the Arts | 147 |

**Appendices**

| | |
|---|---|
| Glossary of Musical Terms | 151 |
| Modes of the Major Scale | 155 |
| Guitar Chord Library | 157 |

# Preface

This book is for the Lord Jesus Christ. It is written in hopes that the worship that ascends to Him will be more excellent, more pleasing to Him and more worthy of who He is and what He has done.

This book is for the Church. It is meant to be a very practical help to those in the ministry of worship and those interested in worship. It is born out of many years of working with congregations and worship teams and seeing the particular needs of these local fellowships. Many of the challenges they face are common. Some of the answers we have found to these common problems are recorded here.

*Because He's Worthy* is not a comprehensive work, indeed it is not meant to be. There are scores of good books on worship that go into more detail than I can offer here and I would refer you to them. What this book *does* offer is a greater understanding of how to make Biblical worship practical in our churches today.

What can we *do today* to increase the scope and effect of our worship? How can we impart the vision in our churches? How can we get from where we are to where we want to go in worship? These questions will be approached both from a scriptural and musical standpoint.

Although much of the material is original, the balance has been gleaned from the teaching of many men and women of God. Acknowledgement must be made to the ministries of Judson Cornwall, Graham Kendrick, John Wimber, Brian Doerksen, Terry Virgo, Steve Griffing and many others who, through different mediums, influenced my life through the years. I pass this along in the same spirit of sharing, in hopes that the Body of Christ will be edified. If it is not possible for you to order other copies, permission is given to copy portions of this work for use in local congregations.

May our praise reflect the beauty and wonder of the magnificent Son of God, *because He's worthy*!

# Section One

# A Biblical Foundation

# What is Worship?

A mother and her young daughter were embarking on the lengthy train ride that would take them to visit a far-off relative. As the passengers settled in for the long haul, the young girl nestled into the window seat and stared in wonderment at the passing objects. "Look mommy, a house!" she exclaimed. "Look mommy, a cow! Mommy, there's a pond! Oh! See the ducks!"

As this went on, the woman became a bit embarrassed at the enthusiasm of her daughter. She turned to those sitting nearby and said, "I'm sorry, my daughter still thinks that everything is wonderful."

Isn't it sad that we who are redeemed and enjoy access to and fellowship with the God of all creation somehow lose the wonder of it all. It is a lifestyle of true worship that creates a wellspring of fresh wonder in our walk with God.

There is no more important calling or duty for us than worship. It is what we were created for and it is our destiny. It is the essence and measure of our relationship with God and the Bible tells us that God is actively seeing those who will worship Him. He is not seeking servants, ministers or workers... He is seeking worshipers!

After years of study, practical experience and teaching on the subject, I still find that worship is quite a difficult thing to define in a simple statement. My best try is: **worship is a revelation and a response.** God's part is to reveal Himself to us. As He reveals Himself and we see Him as He is, our part is to respond to Him by yielding to His majesty and giving our all to Him. It is beholding Him and responding to Him in our hearts, our actions and our way of life. **In short, worship is intimacy with God.** It is receiving His love and loving Him back. Let's take a deeper look at this process of revelation and response.

**A revelation: seeing God as He is**
*("I have heard of Thee by the hearing of the ear, but now my eye sees Thee. Therefore I retract, and I repent in dust and ashes." Job 42:5-6)*

We can only worship God as He reveals His infinite self to us. The half-hearted worship in many churches reflects the degree of revelation the congregation has of God as well as their relationship to Him. A.W. Tozer, in his book *Worship: the missing jewel of the church,* wrote that "worship is pure or base as we entertain high or low thoughts of God." The quality of our worship is directly related to the way we view God. I believe that we can all agree that God is greater than our present understanding of Him.

Many do not worship because they have not seen Him clearly enough. There is a story of an East Indian preacher who went on an excursion to Mount Everest. While with his party, he finally came to the place where they could see the great summit and, while the rest of the party stood transfixed at the sight, he seemed unimpressed. The guide sensed his disappointment and asked him what was the matter. "I suppose I just thought I would see more" he replied. The others were getting restless, so the guide asked him to wait there for about twenty minutes and then catch up with the rest of the party.

## *The quality of our worship is directly related to the way we view God*

As he waited, the mist that covered the mountain, which was barely visible before, began to lift. As it did the preacher said that it was if the mountain took a majestic step forward and he saw the breathtaking magnificence of Everest. To this day that preacher says that "somewhere in the world there is a group of people who were in that party who would say they have seen Mount Everest... I would have to say that they saw nothing." They didn't see the grandeur because they didn't wait long enough.

The tragic parallel to this story is that *so many people don't see the glory and magnificence of God because they don't hang around Him enough to really see Him.* Our worship is limited because our view of God is so limited.

When we consider the character of God in His holiness, complexity, infinity, unchangingness, love, purity, glory, greatness, strength, reliability, wisdom, creativity, availability, generosity, justice, beauty, forgiveness, kindness, power, faithfulness, peacefulness, mercy, stability, patience, victory, goodness, to name a few, we must respond. To the degree that we truly see Him, we truly worship; that much, and no more.

In my personal times of worship I often very quickly run out of words to express what I feel. I realize that my worship vocabulary is limited. As the Holy Spirit guides me in the knowledge of God, my words start to catch up to my current revelation of Him. The more I see Him, the deeper my expression of worship becomes.

Let's take a brief look at two aspects of God's character to see how they effect our worship.

**Holiness:** Holiness is a central attribute of God. It is also something that is difficult for us to relate to. If we speak of the strength of God or the wisdom of God we have earthly examples we can relate to. We all know people who walk in a degree of wisdom or who have a measure of strength. But how do we understand holiness? We have no earthly model of absolute holiness.

When Isaiah had a vision of God did he see the angels around the throne crying "Eternal", "Wise", or "Loving?" No, they cried "Holy, holy, holy is the Lord God Almighty" (See also the scene from heaven in Revelation 5). If we understand this quality of God it will revolutionize our worship.

Basically it means that God is separate. He is other. He is completely and infinitely perfect. He doesn't conform to a holy standard, He *is* the standard. He never does anything wrong. There are no degrees to His holiness. He doesn't grow into it, He *is* it. He is free from any stain, absolutely pristine in His purity. Purity in our worship and our lives comes from understanding His holiness.

This effects how we approach Him. Although He has welcomed us into His presence through the blood of Jesus, we do not go there lightly. He hates our sin. It separates us from Him and we must deal with it if we are to approach Him.

Amos 5:21-23: says *"I hate, I reject your festivals, nor do I delight in your solemn assemblies. Even though you offer up to me burnt offerings and your grain offerings, I will not accept them; and I will not even look at the peace offerings of your fatlings.* ***Take away from me the noise of your songs; I will not even listen to the sound of your harps.***" It's not that God hates music; He hates when the heart of the musician is tainted with sin. We need the fear of the Lord in our worship. He is awesome and holy. We must approach Him that way.

Every time an Old Testament Jew killed and offered a sacrifice, he illustrated the deadliness of sin in contrast to God's holiness. Every time we offer a sacrifice of praise, we must be mindful of God's holiness. This brings a respectful attitude in praise, worship and thanksgiving. It deepens every expression of worship we offer to God. "Worship Him in the beauty of holiness: fear before Him all the earth." (Ps. 96:9)

Until a man knows the holiness of God, he can never understand the depth of his own sin. We cannot be deeply grieved about our own sin if we do not understand the holiness of God. When worship is shallow we do not offer the acceptable sacrifice of a broken and contrite (repentant) spirit and God becomes our good buddy, not our God. In Heb. 12:28 acceptable worship is defined as reverence and godly fear. So we can see how an understanding of His holiness effects our worship.

> *Every time an Old Testament Jew killed and offered a sacrifice, he illustrated the deadliness of sin in contrast to the holiness of God. Every time we offer a sacrifice of praise, we must be mindful of God's holiness.*

**Love:** God's love is foundational to all that He is. He doesn't have love, He *is* love. All that He does flows from and is governed by His essence of love. It is His love which draws us to know Him in the first place. It is eternal, unconditional and ultimately sacrificial. God chose us to be His friend, His child. Dick Eastman, in his book *A Celebration of Praise,* writes: "He chose me having prior knowledge of the worst in me, the worst things I would ever do, so that no discovery can now disillusion Him about me the way I am often disillusioned about myself." Because He is love, He paid the highest price that I might be together with Him. Understanding this truly effects the quality of our worship. We love Him because He first loved us. We worship Him because of His initiating, never-ending love.

By briefly studying these two attributes of God we understand that seeing Him as He has revealed Himself affects the quality of our worship. I believe that one aspect of idolatry is thinking thoughts of God that are untrue of Him. **Is the knowledge of God the primary pursuit of your life? Our worship is only as deep as our revelation of Him.**

**A response: yielding to Him**
*("...offer your bodies as living sacrifices, holy and pleasing unto God – this is your spiritual act of worship." Romans 12:1)*

Yielding to Him is bowing to His awesome and absolute supremacy. It is humbling ourselves. It is understanding who He is and who we are and responding accordingly. It is worshiping Him on His terms.

There is an acceptable way to worship and an unacceptable way to worship. Most of us would not be found bowing before a false God, an idol. However, there are many instances in the Bible of people worshiping the true God in a false way. There were certain prescribed ways by which God was to be approached. When men violated these they oftentimes met judgment. Worshiping Him on His terms means approaching Him on the basis of the sacrifice of Jesus Christ. It means having the right attitude or state of heart. It means realizing that He is God, and we are not.

We have to come to terms with the fact that the God we serve is beyond us. He does things sometimes that are unexplainable to us. If we try to keep Him in a box (presuming to know how He will respond on every occasion) we will be disappointed and we will find that the things He does offend us. We have to recognize that His ways and thoughts are higher than our ways and thoughts.

Worship involves yielding our heart, soul, mind and strength to God. It is a relinquishing of our rights and being conformed to the image of Jesus Christ. It is bowing in response to the awesome greatness of God and cooperating with His dealings. In the very essence of worship there is an attitude of "nevertheless, not my will, but thine be done". That is what makes worship so much more than what goes on in a public gathering. By its very nature true worship requires giving every aspect of your life to God. You cannot give your life to God in one service or in one day. It takes a lifetime to give your life to Jesus.

So worship is a daily walk of obedience and yieldedness to God. It is the natural response of every heart that truly sees God.

*By its very nature true worship requires giving every aspect of your life to God. You cannot give your life to God in one day. It takes a lifetime to give your life to Jesus.*

**A further response: giving our all to Him**
*("...love the Lord your God with all your heart and with all your soul and with all your mind and with all your strength." Mark 12:30)*

It is a revelation to some people to learn that when we come to worship, we come not to get blessed, but to bless God. It is giving, not receiving. Some people approach worship as if it were their birthday, and come away angry if they don't get something out of it. We have to remember that it is not our party! A worship service is not about us and what we receive, it is about God and what *He* receives.

In the Old Testament no one came to worship God without bringing a sacrifice. People did not approach God with the attitude of getting only... they came to give to Him. Many times we reveal our inner attitudes when we say things like "I just didn't get much out of worship this morning" or "We just didn't seem to break through this time." Oftentimes we say this sort of thing never even stopping to realize that God didn't get much out of us this morning either! *It's not about us, it's about Him!* When our focus is on what we get out of it we do not truly worship.

When we speak about giving ourselves to God, we do not mean merely giving an hour or two a week to worship Him... we mean living a lifestyle of bringing honor to God in all that you do. Take a moment to consider what a radical difference it would make in this world if every Christian resolved to live every day from the perspective of "what did God get from me today?" Perhaps at last we would truly be the salt and light we are called to be. That is a lifestyle of worship.


**The purpose of worship: intimacy**
The real purpose of worship is intimacy with God. It has always been His heart to have true fellowship with us. He created us for fellowship. When we fell He redeemed us through Christ so that we could have fellowship with Him. He longs to reveal Himself to us.

Intimacy is always a two-way experience. He draws us to Himself and speaks to us. As we behold His beauty, we fall in love with Him and respond through our gifts of praises, our hearts, and our lives. Our worship is to be a never-ending process of progressive intimacy with the Almighty!

# What Jesus Taught about Worship
## Learning about worship from the One we worship

*Text: John 4:3-26*

*When the Lord learned of this, he left Judea and went back once more to Galilee.*

*Now he had to go through Samaria. So he came to a town in Samaria called Sychar, near the plot of ground Jacob had given to his son, Joseph. Jacob's well was there and Jesus, tired as he was from the journey, sat down by the well. It was about the sixth hour.*

*When a Samaritan woman came to draw water, Jesus said to her, "Will you give me a drink?" (His disciples had gone into the town to buy food.)*

*The Samaritan woman said to him, "You are a Jew and I am a Samaritan woman. How can you ask me for a drink?" (For the Jews do not associate with the Samaritans.)*

*Jesus answered her, "If you knew the gift of God and who it is that asks you for a drink, you would have asked him and he would have given you living water."*

*"Sir," the woman said, "you have nothing to draw with and the well is deep. Where can you get this living water? Are you greater than our father Jacob, who gave us the well and drank from it himself, as did also his sons and his flocks and herds?"*

*Jesus answered, "Everyone who drinks this water will be thirsty again, but whoever drinks the water I give him will never thirst. Indeed, the water I give him will become in him a spring of water welling up to eternal life."*

*The woman said to him, "Sir, give me this water so that I won't have to get thirsty and keep coming here to draw water,"*

*He told her, "Go and call your husband and come back."*

*"I have no husband," she said.*

*Jesus said to her, "You are right when you say you have no husband. The fact is, you have had five husbands, and the man you have now is not your husband. What you have said is quite true."*

*"Sir," the woman said, "I can see that you are a prophet. Our fathers worshiped on this mountain, but you Jews claim that the place where we must worship is in Jerusalem."*

*Jesus declared. "Believe me, woman, a time is coming when you will worship the Father neither on this mountain, nor in Jerusalem. You Samaritans worship what you do not know; we worship what we do know, for salvation is from the Jews. Yet a time is coming and has now come when the true worshipers will worship the Father in Spirit and in truth, for they are the kind of worshipers the Father seeks. God is a Spirit, and his worshipers must worship in spirit and in truth."*

*The woman said, "I know that Messiah" (called Christ) "is coming. When he comes, he will explain everything to us."*

*Then Jesus declared, "I who speak to you and he."*

**Background on the incident**

The northern route from Jerusalem to Galilee (through Samaria) was the shortest, but it was not normally taken by the Jews because they would go many miles out of their way to avoid the Samaritans.

The Samaritans were of mixed descent, being half-Jews. They had once been true Israelites, united with Israel under Saul, David, and Solomon. When the kingdom split, Judah, the southern kingdom, became independent. The northern kingdom, Israel, fell into abominable wickedness and was divinely judged, being captured in 721 B.C. by the Assyrians, under Sargon. All Israel was taken captive and led away into slavery except the poorest people, who represented a burden to the Assyrians. Eventually these remaining poor Jews intermarried with the Babylonians and others. The resulting race was known as Samaritans, named after their capital city, Samaria. They were looked upon by the Jews as half-breeds who had "sold their birthright" and were despised.

This episode reveals the heart of Jesus to reach the "undesirables". God led him where a Jew of that day would not go for a divine appointment. The text says he "had to go through Samaria". He went in order to reveal himself and the Father to a woman through a teaching on worship.


**First things first: the condition of your heart**

When the woman expressed a desire for spiritual things (to partake of the living water that Jesus spoke of) Jesus wasted no time getting to the heart of the matter: her spiritual condition. It was as though He said, "all right, if you want this water you first must deal with the sin in your life. Go call your husband."

If we are to be true worshipers we must first deal with the sin in our lives. I don't know of a single major passage on worship in the Bible that does not also deal, in some way, with the condition of our hearts. God is holy and we are not. Our sins separate us from Him and therefore they must be faced squarely, repented of and forsaken if we are to know Him and worship Him. Repentance is the first step to worship.

Redemption is a foundation of worship. In Revelation chapter 5 we see all the hosts of heaven worshiping Jesus. It is the greatest scene of worship in the Bible. And what are the inhabitants of heaven crying out? They do not say, "worthy is the great king" or, "Worthy is the Lion of the Tribe of Judah". They do not cry out in praise to the "Son of God" or the "King of Kings" or "Lord of Lords", nor do they call Him by any of His other given titles. They cry out "WORTHY IS THE *LAMB* WHO WAS SLAIN!" They worship the Redeemer. Their worship is based on the fact that through the blood of Jesus they are now made right with God.

The Father sent Christ to seek and save us not primarily to deliver us from hell, but for the specific purpose of producing children who would draw near and know Him intimately. Essentially, we are not saved in order for us to receive something, but for God to receive glory from us.

*If we are to be true worshipers we must first deal with the sin in our lives. I don't know of a single major passage on worship in the Bible that doesn't also deal, in some way, with the condition of our hearts.*

Psalm 22 is a Messianic psalm, foretelling of the redeeming death of Jesus. This redemptive psalm ends in the only proper response to His atoning death, *"From Thee comes my praise in the great assembly... those who seek Him will praise the Lord... and all the families of the nations will worship before thee."* The true expression of the redeemed is heartfelt worship to God. One cannot become a true worshiper apart from redemption, and one who is genuinely redeemed becomes a true worshiper.

The normal reaction to the revelation of the Lamb of God is worship. We will worship when we see the fullness of His great redemption. We cannot do anything else.

**It is possible to go through all the outward forms of worship and not *know* the One you are worshiping!**

*"You worship that which you do not know."* What an indictment! May it never be said of us that we are going through the motions of worshiping God and yet we do not even know Him.

When the Samaritans intermarried, their religion became a mixture of Judaism and paganism. Although they seemed to want to maintain their Jewish heritage, the Jews rejected them, so they established their own place of worship, and their own method, building a temple on Mount Gerizim. In 128 B.C. the Maccabean ruler John Hyrcanus destroyed their temple, and although it was never rebuilt, they continued to worship there on Mount Gerizim. To my understanding, there are still some Samaritans around today who still meet on that mountain to worship in their own way independent of Judaism.

The Samaritan woman Jesus spoke to associated worship with a place and a method. She knew of two contrasting forms of worship, her Samaritan way and His Jewish way, and she seemed to be asking Jesus which of the two is the right way.

So her question was, "Which is the right way to worship? Where is the right place? You say it is in Jerusalem, we say it is on this mountain, who is right?" It is a question as old as Genesis, when Cain and Able brought different offerings to worship God.

People can ask similar questions today. With so many forms of worship, whose way is right?

> - You say men should reverence God and worship in silence; we say shout, be free, and express yourself.
> - You say close your eyes and bow your head; we say lift up your eyes, heads and hands to God.
> - You say draw near to God in intimacy; we say storm the gates of hell and take the kingdom by force.
> - You say decently and in order; we say led by the Spirit.

Which way is the right way?

Jesus' answer went basically like this: "Worship is not in outward forms but in an inner relationship." It has to do with truly knowing God and communing with him. Worship is not only a ritual or a set of actions, it is knowing God.

In John 17:3 Jesus said, "*And this is eternal life, that they may know Thee, the only true God, and Jesus Christ whom Thou hast sent.*" Eternal life has to do with knowing God, being intimately acquainted with Him. It is one thing to know about someone, it is quite a different thing to know him or her personally. Many people know nothing about God. Others know a little, and still others know quite a lot of information about Him, but this doesn't necessarily mean that they know Him personally. It is possible to be in the church for many years and have lots of Bible knowledge and yet not know the Father personally. You cannot truly worship Him until you know Him personally.

**We worship the *Father* (vss. 21, 23)**
Jesus said that true worshipers worship the *Father*. This may be the most radical thing he ever said. The concept of God as Father was totally foreign to the Jews, much less the Samaritans. To them God was a distant and unapproachable being who could not be known in a relational sense. He was the Holy One who spoke to Moses from the dark clouds on the mountain. They were so afraid of Him they said to Moses, "You go speak with God. We will not speak to Him." They were forbidden even to utter his name. How could they think of God in terms of a Father? Besides all of this they had over 600 laws, mostly manmade, that kept God at a distance and bound their relationship to Him to a list of do's and don'ts. It was a very impersonal relationship based on performance.

Jesus shattered that false understanding of God. He called God Father, and spoke of God in intimate terms. It was for this reason the Jewish leaders wanted to kill Jesus, because in saying God was his Father, he made himself equal with God (John 10: 22-42).

In his short teaching on worship, Jesus revealed to us the identity of the Object of our worship. God wants us to know that He does not desire to be worshiped from a distance, or be thought of as unapproachable. He wants us to know that He is the Father of all who are saved. He views us as a good and loving father would view his children. He wants to be with us, to protect, provide for and bless us. He is no longer on that mountain amidst the dark clouds and thunderings. We may now draw near through the blood of Christ. Worship is the true revelation of God the Father and of Jesus Christ, his Son, our Savior.

*Jesus said that true worshipers worship the Father.*
*This may be the most radical thing he ever said.*

"Father" was Jesus' favorite title for God, used every time he spoke to God (about 70 times) except when he was on the cross, when, bearing the judgment for our sin, he said, "My God, my God, why have you forsaken me?" In the passage we are studying (John 4) Jesus refers to the Father three times.

It is important to understand that the God we worship is not the same as the gods of the Muslims, the cults, the Jews, or the liberal theologians who deny the deity of Jesus Christ. We worship God, the Father of the Lord Jesus Christ. Jesus declared that he was one with the Father. He is God the Son. Knowing *Who* we worship is extremely important.


**We worship *in spirit***

Jewish worship was highly ritualistic, a very strict liturgical form. It was a certain activity that certain people did in a certain way at a certain prescribed time and place. They accepted all of the Old Testament. They had the truth yet lacked the spirit. They had revelation without life. They were orthodox, but fruitless.

I have been in churches where the Word of God was supreme. They memorized it, studied it painstakingly and taught it faithfully. Even the hymns they sung were full of theology. Yet there was very little life. They held to the Word while denying the working of the Spirit. They loved the letter of the law, but not the spirit of the law.

Notice what Jesus said in John 5:39:

*"You diligently study the Scriptures because you think that by them you possess eternal life. These are the Scriptures that testify about me, yet you refuse to come to me to have life."*

The Word of God is a living Word, active and powerful. When we are passionate about our doctrine, or about being "right", instead of passionate for Christ, we are in error.

On the opposite extreme, I have been in churches where the emotions that came from zealous worship reigned supreme. The feelings were lord over the truth, and this can lead to error, if not heresy.

The Samaritans had a limited understanding of God because they rejected all of the Old Testament except for the Pentateuch (the first five books of the Old Testament). They had enthusiastic worship without the proper information. They had passion without truth. It was zealous worship done in ignorance.

Both ways are wrong. Jesus tells us that we must worship in spirit *and* in truth. He also warned the Sadducees in Matthew 22:29, *"You are in error because you do not know the Scriptures or the power of God."* We must have both sound Biblical truth and the powerful, living presence of the Spirit of God in our worship. To exclude either is to be in error.

So how do we worship in spirit? That seems to be such an ambiguous phrase. What does it mean? I think that it first means that worship has to come from the inside, not just from the mouth. Secondly, it must be enthusiastic. Why do we smile? Why do we clap and lift our hands and dance? Because we know God and we recall His great mercy toward us and we are glad! When our heart is full it overflows.

Even if we have much knowledge about God, as the Pharisees did, and if we pray and fast and give alms, but not from the heart, we are, as they were, hypocrites and full of dead men's bones. Isaiah prophesied of a people who "honor [God] with their lips, but their heart is far away from [God]."

The word 'spirit' used here means the human spirit. Worship has to come from the inside out. It takes place on the inside and is then manifested on the outside. God's primary concern is the inside, not the outside. When our hearts are so sincerely full of the beauty and wonder of God that it spills out our mouths we are truly worshiping.

**We worship *in truth***

I think worshiping in truth has at least two meanings. First it means that our worship is based on the unchanging truth of the Word of God.

* The truth is that He is God and we are not.
* The truth is that God is righteous and holy and just in all His ways.
* The truth is that He has redeemed us from every tongue and tribe and made us kings and priests unto Himself.
* The truth is that He calls us to draw near to Him with hearts full of faith being washed clean on our evil consciences.
* The truth is that if we confess our sins, He is faithful and just to forgive us our sins and cleanse us from all unrighteousness.
* The truth is that the Lamb who was slain is worthy to receive power and riches and wisdom and strength and honor and glory and blessing!

We must worship based on truth, and not based on how we feel at the moment. God is still worthy, no matter how we feel. Our feelings are fickle and let us down constantly. The truth of God must be our rock and our fortress in such times.

Secondly I believe worshiping in truth means that we are true to the state of our hearts. Man looks on the outward but God looks on the inside. It is God who tries the heart. He knows the content and state of our heart. We cannot fool Him. In Psalm 51 David tells us that God desires truth in the inner person. We must be sincere in our worship.

There is a story behind the word "sincere" that illustrates my point. It is said that the word originally came from two different words: *sin*, meaning "without"; and *cera*, meaning "wax". When certain potters would spin a clay pot and fire it, at times cracks would appear in the product. Instead of discarding the pot, the merchant would melt wax, pour it into the cracks, smooth them over, and paint or glaze it as though it were a perfectly good pot. The unsuspecting buyer would not know the difference until he got it home and put it to the fire and the pot would promptly break. The pot was not in reality what it appeared to be. I believe this is one part of what Jesus meant when he spoke of worshiping in truth. We must worship without wax. If your heart is far far from God, don't pretend that it isn't. If you are afraid or angry, in your heart, don't pretend that you are not.

David was a man who came before the Lord and told him just how he felt. In the third Psalm, he was completely in despair, surrounded by his enemies and meditating on his own calamity. He didn't hide it from God. He had an honest relationship with God.

He told God how he felt. Then God strengthened him and encouraged him. And this scene is repeated many times in the Psalms. In Psalm 22 David cries out in utter despair and God turns his song into a prophecy concerning the coming Messiah!

In Psalm 73, Asaph is mad and distracted almost to the point of falling away from God because he sees the prosperity of the wicked. He came to the point of believing that it is vanity to serve God. He did not hide that from God. Indeed he could not. God already knew his heart.

Because he was truthful in his heart before God, God gave him the right perspective. The end of the wicked is utter destruction. When Asaph saw this he realized how out of hand he had been in presuming injustice upon God. When we are truthful in our hearts before God, He begins to help us see straight. Psalm 145:8 says, "The Lord is near to all who call upon Him, to all who call upon Him in truth."

**God seeks worshipers**

Jesus ended his teaching on worship with an amazing statement: "Yet a time is coming and has now come when the true worshipers will worship the Father in spirit and truth, *for they are the kind on worshipers the Father seeks.*"

Consider this statement. What does God need? What could be so all-important, so precious that the all-powerful, all-knowing, all-inclusive God of the universe would seek after it? Is He not sufficient in Himself? Yet we are told that God is looking for something.

Why do you search for something? Because it is precious to you? Because you lost it? Because you want or need it? And God, we are told, is seeking those who would worship Him the right way. He is searching for true worshipers. This reveals the importance of our worship to God. Not because He is an ego-maniac, or so insecure that He needs people around to tell Him how great He is, but because He longs for communion with those whom He created and redeemed. He loves us. He created and redeemed us for the purpose of worship and communion with Him. That was His one desire. That is why He is seeking worshipers. Will you say, "Here I am, Lord, I will be the worshiper you seek?"

# What Happens When We Worship

God is a living God and His Word is active and powerful. Things happen when we encounter Him. Worship is a dynamic experience. When we worship Him He is active on our behalf. I believe that God is always desiring to reveal Himself and interact with His people and that worship produces an atmosphere which makes that possible. It allows us the opportunity to open our hearts, to pour out our love to Him, to be more aware of Him and sensitive to His voice.

In this section we will consider some of the things that take place when we worship. As we do we will learn at least six of the primary purposes of music.

| What Happens When We Worship | Corresponding God-Ordained Purpose for Music |
|---|---|
| We Glorify God | A Vehicle of Praise and Worship |
| The Church Is Edified | Teaching and Encouragement |
| God Fights for Us | Spiritual Warfare |
| God Speaks to Us | Prophetic Expression |
| God Sets Us Free | Supernatural Deliverance |
| The Lost Are Reached | Revealing God |

**We glorify God**

The Bible tells us that all things were created for God's pleasure (Rev. 4:11). When we worship we have the extraordinary privilege of bringing Him pleasure! It is incredible to think that we can actually make Him smile. The lesser can bless the Greater. My personal worship experience was transformed when I realized that my worship and prayers actually ascend to the throne of God as sweet smelling incense, a tangible expression that brings Him pleasure. I make Him smile!

Worship is ascribing glory to God. Psalm 50:23 says, "Whoever offers praise glorifies me." When we praise we join the hosts of heaven and all creation in recognizing God's glory and applauding Him for it.

Psalm 29:2 says that we are to give God "the glory due to His name." The word "glory" literally means "weight" in the original Hebrew. In that light, we can visually interpret Psalm 29:2 by thinking of a scale. On one side we put all the infinite worth of the Almighty: His character, His works, His ways, His intrinsic greatness. The scale immediately plunges to one side. Our job, in giving Him the glory due to His Name, is to offer Him praise that is equal to His value in order to balance the scale again. Of course we come tragically short in our effort; nonetheless, this should be our goal.

*Worship is such a deeply satisfying experience because in it we are doing the very thing we were created to do.*

In the Bible we are told that all creatures in heaven and earth as well as under the earth will recognize the worthiness of Christ and respond in praise (Phil. 2:10-11; Rev. 5:12-13). Tragically, man in his selfish existence and his sinful state fails to see the obvious. It is possible to live our hurried lives long without stopping to even acknowledge the glory, holiness and worthiness of God Almighty. Worship therefore, is, among other things, a reality check. It allows us to adjust our thinking and see God as He is. We see His majesty and we respond by glorifying Him. God is honored in our worship.

Music has power to sway our passions and affections. Advertising agencies have known this for years. It works, or they wouldn't spend billions of dollars a year to do it. Ask me to memorize the ingredients of your product and I'll say, "You're crazy!" But put those ingredients to a catchy tune and play it enough times and I'll be singing the praise of your product, whether I like it or not!

The great composers knew how to use the ability of music to sway emotions to their advantage. In Mozart's day, it was common practice to take the listener on an excursion through many different emotions in a single piece of music. That is why Mozart's music in just five minutes draw you through feelings of majesty, melancholy, light-hearted joy, rage, peace and on and on. It was no different in David's day. The superscriptions we see written at the beginning of most of the Psalms contain musical terms that seem to refer to the style or idiom of the music to which the Psalm was set. We can be quite sure that lamenting music was used for laments, joyous music for celebrations, and so on. Music has the power to move the hearer.

God wants to gather our passion and adoration and focus them on Him through music. Psalm 150 says, *"You* praise the Lord" -- in every place, for all things, on every kind of musical instrument -- "let everything that has breath, praise the Lord!" All things were made for the purpose of glorifying God. Bringing Him glory is our chief end and the thing we were created for, and we are accomplishing that when we worship. That is why true worship is such a deeply satisfying experience. We are doing the very thing we were created to do.

**The church is edified**

As we worship we are built up in Christ and transformed. "As we behold Him, we are changed from glory to glory" (2 Cor. 3:18). *If you read the book of Acts, you find that when the church was worshiping, they enjoyed the favor of the Lord, the Lord added to their number daily, and they made a tremendous impact on their city and the world. They had power and were attractive to the world.*

The general ministry of the Holy Spirit is to glorify Jesus, to teach us about Him, to edify us and encourage us to growth. He does this through direct revelation of the Word of God. He does it through the gifts of the Spirit. He also does it through music as we worship. We are all witnesses to this fact. How many times have we been deeply encouraged or shown a new aspect of God's character by a song (see 1 Cor. 14:26)?

*Edification isn't just about feeling better, but living better. If the corporate worship in the church leaves people unchanged, the people are not really worshiping.*

Colossians. 3:16 says that we teach and admonish one another through *songs, hymns, and spiritual songs*. Paul uses the same three words in Ephesians 5:19 to show us a progression God often uses to encourage us in worship services. Although it is not a hard and fast rule, there is some validity to the concept that this may be a sort of divine order for worship.

| **Psalms** "Psalmos" | **Hymns** "Humnos" | **Spiritual Songs** "Ode Pneumatica" |
|---|---|---|
| About God | To God | From God |
| Flow of Worship Horizontal | Flow of Worship Ascending | Flow of Worship Descending |
| Celebration of God | 1st Step in Intimacy | 2nd Step in Intimacy |

*Psalms (Gk. psalmos)* : *a sacred song with musical accompaniment. The word seems to denote a song <u>about</u> God,* with which the congregation celebrates God. Many of what we call hymns today are actually psalms in the sense that Paul uses the word here. They speak of God, His greatness, His works, and His characteristics. Examples would include: *Amazing Grace, Awesome God)*

*Hymns (Gk. humnos)* : a *song directed to God*. This is very different from a psalm. Instead of the congregation singing together about God, it becomes personal, with the worshiper singing directly to God. This is the beginning of intimacy, which is the goal of all our worship. Some songs may start out as psalms (sung about God) and end up as hymns (sung to God). Oftentimes you will find an increase in the intensity of worship when you "personalize" a song, singing it to God in first person rather than singing about Him. Examples of hymns would include:
*I Love You Lord, Lord I Lift Your Name On High, Great is Thy Faithfulness*


*Spiritual songs (Gk. ode pneumatikos)* : *literally a song of the Spirit. A spirit-breathed or spirit-inspired song.* This is a song that the Holy Spirit inspires in the heart of a worshiper. In 1 Corinthians 14:15 Paul calls it singing with the spirit. It is the second step in intimacy as God speaks back to us what is on His mind. This may be a spontaneously composed song or a previously composed song which God is using to speak His specific word to an individual or gathering of believers. In this sense, it is a prophetic song. It should not surprise us that, as we sing to the Lord, tenderly expressing our love and adoration to Him, He would want to sing back to us. After all, He said He would (Zeph. 3:17; Heb. 2:11-12).

The first recorded song in the Bible, Exodus 15, bears studying because it actually begins as a "psalm," works it's way into a "hymn" and then ends as a powerful prophetic "spiritual song".

As Moses and the children of Israel came through the Red Sea, being delivered from the bondage of Egypt and the danger of the pursuing army of Pharaoh, a spontaneous song of praise broke out. Verses 1-5 is a very descriptive account of what God has done, who He is, and why they sang this song of celebration (PSALM).

In verse six, the song turns into first person, speaking to God about what He had done and praising Him: *"Who among the gods is like You, O Lord? Who is like You – majestic in holiness, awesome in glory, working wonders?"* (HYMN)

Then in verses 13-18 the song turns into a prophetic proclamation of what God would do now for His people: *"In Your unfailing love You will lead... in Your strength You will guide them into Your holy dwelling. The nations will hear and tremble... Canaan will melt away; terror and dread will fall upon them... they will be as still as a stone until Your people pass by... You will bring them in and plant them on the mountain of Your inheritance... the Lord will reign forever and ever."* (PROPHETIC SONG FROM THE SPIRIT)

**So we see a progression of worship from celebration to adoration to revelation.** The "spiritual song" is really about is a prophetic presence in our worship which flows out of this intimacy with God. Let's explore this area more as we look at another thing that happens when we worship.

**God speaks to us – releasing the prophetic anointing**

God is eternal past and future, but He is also a God of the now. He longs to speak in this moment (His Word is both *logos* and *rhema*). A prophetic anointing is basically God's particular word for a particular people at a particular time. The prophetic word, whether spoken or sung, cuts like a knife through the religious muck that surrounds our hearts, pierces through into our spirit with undeniable power and accuracy and brings the life and purposes of God into focus for us. It also edifies, exhorts and comforts.

Historically, when God wanted to proclaim His specific word to a people, one major way He did it is through music. Many of the Old Testament prophecies were delivered by song. That was a deeply ingrained part of Hebrew culture.

The Hebrew prophets were also the passers on of the Hebrew culture, and they did this through song. They were trained to communicate through music (see Ps.136; 137; 1 Sam. 10 5-6). In 1 Chronicles 25:1-3, David set up a liturgical order of priests who were to "prophesy on their instruments."

One example of this is 2 Kings 3:15 where Elisha, when called upon by kings to prophesy to them, called for a musician to play. When the musician played, the man of God began to prophesy. Also the entire third chapter of Habakkuk is a prophetic prayer set to music and accompanied by stringed instruments. Many of the Psalms begin either as complaints or praises and evolve into prophetic statements about an individual or a nation or even Messianic prophecies foretelling the birth, life, death and resurrection of Jesus! God uses music to prophesy!

Remembe Revelation 19:10: "the testimony of Jesus is the Spirit of prophecy"

See *"Practical tips for Prophetic Worship"*, page 141, for more on this subject.


**God fights for us**

Every time believers gather together and join in triumphant declaration of the supremacy of our Lord the kingdom of darkness suffers great loss. Chains are broken, captives are freed, and the Spirit of God enlightens, convicts and draws men to Jesus. Faith is released in the hearts of believers through music that boldly declares the gospel.

Psalm 149 tells us that praise is a powerful weapon to be used in battle against the enemies of God's kingdom. By praising God we are executing judgment on the forces of darkness, the judgment that Jesus sealed through his death and resurrection. This is an honor that every Christian has. For it was for this very purpose Christ came : "to destroy the works of the devil" (1 John 3:8).

2 Chronicles 20 shows us how this works. Judah was surrounded by enemies. Three kingdoms had come out against them. They didn't know what to do. King Jehoshaphat called a national fast to pray and seek God. "We don't know what to do, but our eyes are on You" was their confession.

God responded, "The battle is not yours, but mine. Stand still and see the salvation of God... go out tomorrow against them." He also gave them specific insight as to how the enemy would attack them. *But how do you stand still and go out at the same time?* Here is how Jehoshaphat responded:

"As we believe what the Lord has said, so shall we prosper." And he appointed a choir of worshipers to go before the army to sing praise to the God who would deliver them. Their praise didn't win the battle, but it was a declaration of faith in the God who would win the battle!

*"And when they began to sing and to praise, the Lord set a trap for the enemy and they all began to kill one another."* Great treasures were captured and the praise had just begun! The fear of God came on all the nations around Judah, because the Lord fought for them. In the same way, the Lord fights for us when we keep our eyes on Him and worship Him.

**Supernatural deliverance**

In 1 Samuel 16:14-23, the Spirit of the Lord had departed from Saul and an evil spirit was tormenting him. Saul's servants suggested that they should find a man who was a "cunning player on the harp" so that when he played for Saul, the evil spirit would leave him. So they found David and that is exactly what happened. *Not only does music tame the savage soul, it drives out the demons that cause the soul to be savage!*

Darkness and sin cannot stay in the presence of God. When we worship God, the forces of darkness must leave! But there were prerequisites for David to be used this way:

1) David was an upright man whom the Lord was with. There is no escaping the fact that our hearts must be right with God (1 Samuel 16:18).

2) David had a secret walk with God. Where do you suppose these men had seen David and heard him play? What had he been doing up to this point? He was a shepherd. He had been singing those songs to his sheep and to his Lord (Psalm 23). He did not start out with a public ministry. He was faithful and walked with his Lord in private. The power comes from a secret walk with God.

3) David was skillful on his instrument. Psalm 33:3 says, "play skillfully, with a loud noise" (excellently, with confidence). David's appointed tabernacle musicians were skillful in the songs of the Lord. Skill brings beauty, clarity, expression, liberty, and authority to our worship. It is worth remembering that we are confined to our limitations on our instruments. The more skillful we are, the freer we are to worship and be used of God.
The role of skill in worship is discussed in more detail in the section entitled *"Seven spirits of a worshiper"*, on page 31

We cannot expect to just pick up an instrument and play and see demons flee. They don't flee from the music, they flee from the presence of God flowing through a consecrated musician who is full of integrity.

**The lost are reached**

Redemption is the foundation of worship (Rev. 4-5). A person or a church that truly worships will have a profound influence on sinners. In the past few years there has been a move of God, especially in non-Christian countries, as Christians have set up simple outdoor concerts of worship in the streets and God has drawn lost to Himself as they experience His presence.

When the unsaved come into contact with the presence of God, oftentimes the outcome is that they sense their deep need for a restored relationship to God. As the Holy Spirit draws them, they can respond to that desire for intimacy with the Father. There have been many times in my experience when people would respond in some form of repentance (coming forward to an altar to pray, sob with deep repentance, and so on) while the congregation was experiencing anointed worship.

David wrote, *"He put a new song in my mouth, a hymn of praise to our God. Many will see and fear and put their trust in the Lord"* (Ps. 40:3). Let us not underestimate the desire of God to touch the hearts of others while we are seeking to touch His heart.

# Seven Spirits of a Worshiper

There are certain heart attitudes that are essential to true worship. That is not to say that everyone who is involved in the worship ministry will be perfected in all of these qualities, but be assured that the Spirit of God will be pro-active in seeing to it that these attitudes are worked into your character as you walk the walk of worship.

**A spirit of humility - slaying the giant of pride**
Pride is a thorn in the flesh of everyone. It is a universal scourge that afflicts the heart of every person. It is the reason for the fall of Satan and, ultimately, the fall of man. We are all vulnerable to it, but if you take a person who has a musical gift and put that person up on a platform in front of others (who do not have the same gift) in a position of authority or importance and on top of that add the dimension of appearing to be very spiritual (after all, anyone who leads worship *must* be more spiritual than those who don't, right?), you have a powder keg of potential pride ready to explode.

The Bible says sobering things about pride. Proverbs 16:18 says that "pride goes before destruction and a haughty spirit before a fall". Psalm 138:6 says that "the proud He knows from afar." In other words, pride separates you from God. If you are feeling far away from God, perhaps the problem is pride. God says that He opposes or resists those who are proud (1 Pet. 5:5). Now if there is one person I don't want to be fighting against, it is God! Perhaps the most sobering scripture about pride is Proverbs 16:5, which says "Every one that is proud in heart is an abomination to the Lord." Even if we are leading worship and trying to draw near to God, we can in fact be an abomination to Him (the very thing that He hates the most) if we are proud in heart.

*If you take a person who has a musical gift and put that person on a platform in front of others in a position of authority or importance and on top of that add the dimension of appearing to be very spiritual, you have a powder keg of potential pride ready to explode.*

So how do we avoid this terrible sin, this destruction, this separation from God? By a lifestyle of humility. A simple study of the Bible references to humility will reveal that to the humble God grants salvation, the nearness of his presence, grace, wealth, honor, life, a revived spirit; and he promises that he will dwell in the hearts of the humble. All of us will sign up for that! But practically speaking, what does it mean to walk in humility?

Humility was embodied in the Lord Jesus Christ. Philippians 2 encourages us to have the same mind that Jesus had. So what kind of mind was that? Although he was equal with God, he didn't grasp after that equality as the thing that was important to him or that gave him worth. Rather, he let his importance go and emptied himself over and over again, even to the point of dying the worst kind of death for the sake of saving us.

Likewise, we need to beware of grasping our position on the worship team as though that is where our importance, significance or identity lies. That kind of insecurity can breed jealousy and an unhealthy inclination to hold on to our "position of ministry" instead of humbling ourselves to serve others.

How does humility work itself out practically in our relationships? We see humility in the attitude of doing whatever needs to be done, not just what we want to do. We see humility in respecting others by coming to practices and services on time. Humility is evident in those who will remain faithfully where they are until they are "called up higher" into another aspect of ministry. Humility shines through the life of a person who refrains from publicly expressing an opinion or "suggestion" about everything, and instead reserves that thought for the appropriate time. Humility blends in, harmonizes and doesn't need to stand out in the group. It is interested in making "one voice to give praise and thanks to the Lord" (2 Chron. 5:13).

This is the spirit of a worshiper: doing what we do, not out of selfishness or personal ambition, but considering others better than ourselves. Not looking to our own interests, but rather thinking of others. It is humility before God and before others. It is emptying ourselves out for the sake of our king, our brothers and sisters and the world.

There is another, subtle form of pride that should be addressed: those who feign humility and mask their pride by saying, "Oh, I'm not really that good," or, "I could never do a solo." The real issue in this sort of pride is not wanting to step out and possibly make a mistake; not wanting to be seen as inferior or less than perfect. It is a dangerous sort of pride which suppresses giftings and causes individuals and worship teams to linger in mediocrity instead of pressing on to excellence.

We need to have a realistic view of who we are and the gifts that God has given us. Romans 12:3 tells us that we should not think of ourselves more highly than we ought to think. In other words, don't have too high an estimation of your worth, but don't think too lowly either. God *has* gifted us. But it is *God* who gifted us, not we ourselves. Because of our tendency toward sin, the very gifts that God blesses us with can turn into the things that we idolize and lead us away from him.

For example, when Moses encountered God at the burning bush, God asked him to do something that tested his trust. Moses had already been broken by forty years of herding sheep. Now he was standing in the awesome presence of God Almighty, facing one more test. *God asked Him to throw down his rod.* Now a rod was just about all that a shepherd had. It was his identity, his security, his authority, his protection and the tool of his trade. In other worsds, God was asking Moses "Will you lay down all that you have, all that you are before me?"

*The rod in Moses' hands was good for nothing but herding sheep. But in the hands of God there was no limit to what could be done. What rod do you hold in your hand?*

When Moses made the decision to lay it down a strange thing happened. The rod became a serpent, a fearful and dangerous thing. Moses ran when he saw it. Then God asked him to do an even stranger thing; pick the serpent up by the tail! Moses stepped up and did it and the serpent became a rod again. However it was not the same rod. Before it had been the rod of Moses. From now on it would be called the *rod of God*. It was the rod of God that was stretched out to call forth the incredible plagues upon the Egyptians. It was the rod of God with which God parted the Red Sea and brought forth water from the rock. That rod, in Moses' hands, was good for nothing but herding sheep. But in the hands of God there was no limit to what could be done.

Ask yourself the same question that God asked Moses: "What do you have in your hand?" What has God given to you that you have not surrendered up for His purposes? Many times we discover that the very gifts of God, in our hands, are fearful and dangerous. They can become idols. They can steal glory from God by drawing attention to themselves. When we truly give them to God, lay them down at his feet and then pick them up again, we see that there is great freedom, great power and great blessing for His kingdom.

**The spirit of a servant – one under authority**

Akin to the spirit of humility is the spirit of a servant. It is imperative that those of us who are Christians (and especially those who aspire to ministry in the house of the Lord) must constantly press ourselves into the mold of the One whom we worship. Jesus gave us his job description in his own words in Matthew 20:28 "The Son of Man did not come to be served, but to serve, and to give his life as a ransom for many." We must ask ourselves honestly: do we have an attitude of serving the body or do we look to be served?

The Levites in the Old Testament were always ready to do their job, but they were also willing to do whatever task they were assigned. The call to the ministry of worship is not solely for our enjoyment or to make us feel important in our position in the church. We are not set up front to look pretty, but we are called to serve the people that we lead in worship. We must be that committed to the body we are a part of. We must have a burden to see God's purposes fulfilled in the saints, praying for them to grow in the knowledge of the Lord Jesus. Without this understanding our ministry can become mundane and we lose our perspective. Take a moment to think. Do those around you see you as a servant? In what ways can you practically serve those to whom you are ministering?

*The call to the ministry of worship is not solely for our enjoyment or to make us feel important about our position in the church. We are not set up front to look pretty, but we are called to serve the people that we lead in worship.*

Another aspect of service is one's attitude toward those in charge. In 1 Chronicles 25 we find a definite authority structure in the system of Levitical worship set up by David. It looked something like this:

# 4,000 Levite musicians/singers

were under the hand of

# 288 specially trained teachers
### (the sons of Asaph, Heman, and Jeduthun)

were under the hand of

### their fathers
### (Asaph, Heman and Jeduthun)

were under the hand of

# David, the King

      Authority is important to God. There is a recurrent theme throughout the scriptures concerning God's blessing on those who are submitted to God-ordained authority. There is protection, anointing and a maturing process that comes from being submitted to those whom God has put over us. With the calling comes the wisdom and sometimes those in authority see things that we are blind to simply because God has given them wisdom to lead.

      Jesus commended a man who had a great understanding of authority as being someone who had the greatest faith in all of Israel (Matt. 8:5-13). Jesus himself submitted to his earthly authorities (his parents) and in doing so matured mentally, spiritually, physically, and socially (Lk. 2:52). David recognized Saul's authority even when Saul's heart was far from the purposes of God, and he said, "I will not lift my hand against God's anointed" (1 Sam. 26:11)

      It is characteristic of a godly minister to submit to those God has placed over him. Whether it is your worship team leader, a pastor or elder, or some other authority, often times you will have to bypass your feelings and emotions, have a Gethsemane experience, and say, "nevertheless, not my will, but yours." That is not to say that there is no place for a godly appeal. Leadership is not perfect either, and sometimes an appeal is in order. The point is that a servant spirit recognizes authority and responds appropriately to it.

**The spirit of a warrior - the other side of authority**

Many of us fall short of what God desires for us because we do not understand the authority that he has given to us. God doesn't want us just to sing and play; he wants us to sing and play with authority.

One thing that set Jesus apart from the religious teachers of his day was that he taught as one who had authority (Matt. 7:29). He knew that He was sent from God - anointed with a mission - and his confidence was based on that truth. In fact, he said that *all* authority in heaven and earth was given to him. What a statement! But then in the very next verse he says to us "Go therefore..." He sends us in his authority! When Jesus sent out his disciples in Luke 9:1, he gave them power to drive out demons and to heal diseases. And again, in Luke 10:19, he says that he gives us authority over all the power of the enemy. He doesn't leave us to minister in our own strength. He has given us spiritual authority.

This has been a liberating truth to me personally. I am generally a laid back person. I am not, by nature, an aggressive, confronting person. But every personality type has its strengths and weaknesses. One of the weaknesses of mine is that I have a tendency to not press in and go for it. There are times that I need to press in and follow the lead of the Holy Spirit in a worship service. There are also times when I don't feel particularly capable or spiritually sensitive. It is at these times I need to rest in the authority that God has given me to function in my calling.

In 2 Corinthians, Paul admits that even he felt inadequate for the ministry he was called to do. When we feel this way we are able to say with Paul, "Not that we are competent in ourselves to claim anything for ourselves, but our competence comes from God" (2 Cor. 3:5). When we are sure of our calling, we can be sure that God's grace and authority is with us to help us in that calling.

Practically speaking, it is impossible to minister with authority as a musician or vocalist without having a degree of skill on your instrument. Those who are proficient on their instruments hold a confidence which allows them to press in and minister effectively.

Three necessary elements in the ministry of worship are ability, anointing and authority. When these elements are balanced it makes for an effective ministry. When they are out of balance, there are potential problems.

**Ability** can also be called talent or gifting. Some people have a natural inclination toward singing, playing an instrument, working with people or worship leading. Obviously we need people of ability in the worship ministry.

However, when the focus is only on *ability* (neglecting anointing and authority) there is a tendency to be polished but not spiritual; showy and even proud, but with no power. You get a good show but there is no effect for the kingdom of God.

**Anointing** is the sanction and presence of God which enables us to do something with a supernatural effect for the kingdom of God. God punctuates our efforts with the power of His Spirit and makes them supernaturally effective.

However, when the focus is only on *anointing* (neglecting ability and authority) you tend to "rely on the Spirit" to the exclusion of your own responsibility to be a good steward of the gift of God. Your ignorance and ineptness can actually hinder you from experiencing the anointing which you desire so much.

**Authority** is the natural and spiritual influence and weightiness that comes from the ability to skillfully handle or execute your particular gifting.

When you focus only on *authority* (neglecting ability and anointing) you tend to minister in the power of the arm of the flesh, being pushy and presumptuous in your gift.

When these three are in *balance*, however, excellent, expressive, sensitive and worship draws the worshiper near to God, and we have worship that enhances and advances the kingdom of God.


**A spirit of excellence - the role of skill in worship**
Throughout the scriptures we see that the men whom God used greatly were men with an excellent spirit. The church is a place where excellence should be the norm. Unfortunately, for various reasons, the church has by and large settled for mediocrity in many areas, music perhaps being a chief one. An attitude of "it's good enough for church" has prevailed. Oh, how we need worshipers that will bring excellence back into the church.

Skill plays a vital role in anointed worship. Psalm 33:3 says to "play skillfully with a loud noise." The musicians appointed by David were described as "cunning" or "skillful" on their instruments. Hebrew tradition and the scriptural accounts of the Levitical priesthood reveal that the Levites began their preparatory training at five years of age. At 25 years old they were introduced to service in the temple and at 30 years old they were fully administering the duties of a priest. At 50 years of age they "retired" and became teachers of the next generation of ministers. So we find that they had roughly twenty years of training; twenty years of service, and then lived out the rest of their years in their *ultimate call -- releasing others into the ministry.*


*Our diligent work to achieve excellence increases the anointing of God and His ability to work through us.*


Although access to the presence of God is not by works, we are told to do everything we do with all of our hearts, as unto the Lord (Col. 3:23). The plain fact is that our diligent work to achieve excellence increases the anointing of God and His ability to work through us.

Let me use myself as an example. I am formally trained on the guitar and the piano. I have a reasonable degree of skill on these instruments, I feel confident on them, and I believe that the Lord can flow through me when I play them. On the other hand, if I tried to pick up a trumpet or saxophone -- no matter how much anointing I feel or how intense the desire and expression of the Holy Spirit is within me -- I promise you, barring a mighty miracle, I would not bless anybody! Instead, I am sure I would hinder the work of the Holy Spirit. Does this mean that I'm not anointed? No, it means that I cannot play the trumpet!

So we see that skill and the anointing work together in the worship ministry. Consider the following facts:

### *Skill brings beauty and excellence to our worship*

Our God is beautiful beyond description. His ways, his character, his very essence is beautiful. We are to worship Him in the *beauty* of His holiness. It is through skill, that is, learning to master our voices and instruments, that our worship reveals the beauty of God, making Him appealing to believers and unbelievers alike. We are bound in our expression of God (and our expression to God) by our limitations on our instruments. As our level of ability increases so the depth and beauty of our worship increases.

### *Skill brings breadth and clarity of expression to our worship*

The greater your proficiency on your instrument, the greater the variety of musical styles and idioms that are at your call in worship. Sadly, most worship teams are tied down to a few styles of worship music, and thus their expression of God is handicapped. Many musicians are like children; they only eat what they like. Most amateur musicians do not know what they like; they like what they know. They are comfortable with what they can play and seldom venture outside that domain. Hence, they are hopelessly bound to a rut of mediocrity because they will not humble themselves, discipline themselves and learn other styles.

God is manifold in His personality and His revelation of Himself. In the Word we see His majesty, holiness, mystery, awesomeness, joy, wrath, strength, lovingkindness and on and on.

What does majesty sound like? What does joy or peace sound like? Can you make those sounds using your voice or instrument? Learning the particulars of your instrument in order to control dynamics, articulation, phrasing, and so on, help to bring contrast and clarity to your worship.

Every singer and musician should be actively seeking to better their musical abilities. Taking private lessons, listening critically to recordings of other excellent musicians, and seeking opportunities to play or sing with those who are further advanced than you, are great places to start.

### *Skill reflects the cost and value of true worship*

Our goal is to give God the caliber of praise that He is worthy of. Wimpy worship is for wimpy gods. Our God deserves the very best! In 2 Samuel 24:24 Araunah offered to give David a parcel of land on which to offer sacrifice to the Lord. David's response is indicative of a true worshiper: I will not offer up to God that which cost me nothing. God gives the talent, but not the skill. The skill costs something. And a true worshiper doesn't offer God something that costs him nothing.

*God gives the talent, but not the skill. Skill costs something... the Holy Spirit is not a labor saving device, and the sovereignty of God does not release us from artistic training.*

Where does one draw the line between diligent application and study on an instrument and relying on the Spirit? I don't think a line needs to be drawn, rather we need a good blend of perspiration and inspiration. The sovereignty of God doesn't release us from artistic training. Of course we don't neglect or belittle the work of the Holy Spirit. But as one man has well said: "The Holy Spirit is not a labor saving device!" True worship costs something and skill is the price that must be paid for excellent worship.

### Skill brings liberty in worship
A person who is in bondage to the mechanics of his instrument cannot hear the Spirit. Lack of skill produces timidity on our instruments and hinders prophetic worship. I encourage the members of the worship teams that I work with to practice the songs until they get them "under their fingers" and to memorize the words and music so that they are not tied down to a page and thus find it impossible to worship God.

In Ezekiel 44 calls those who minister before the Lord to wear nothing that will make them sweat. In the same way, we should work to achieve a level of ability on our instruments so that no matter what the musical situation we are in we can respond by saying "No sweat!"

### Skill brings authority to worship
Kenaniah was given the responsibility of being head of singers because he was skillful at it (1 Chron. 15:22). Skill set him in a place of authority. When you hear someone skillful on their instrument you can feel the authority of God flowing from them. We spoke earlier about authority in worship. Skill is what releases that authority.

### The pursuit of skill produces Christian character
The years of consistent and diligent practice required to become skillful brings about the character qualities of discipline, self-control, and patience. Skill involves the mind, and one who worships without his mind is not a complete worshiper (Matt 22:37). An unskilled worshiper is only one-half of a worshiper.

The pursuit of skill also requires the quality of humility, as the person seeking to better himself must admit that he doesn't know it all and bring himself under the hands of someone better than himself in order to learn. He must say "You are better than me, please teach me."

Understanding of the role of skill in anointed worship should challenge us to abandon mediocrity. Ultimately, God is worthy of the very best we can give him.

**A spirit of sensitivity - having ears to hear**

As we have already learned, one of the primary functions of music as God created it is prophecy. That has to do with being sensitive the Spirit of God in a given situation and responding to what you hear. If we are to work together with the Holy Spirit, we must apply ourselves to listen and express what we hear.

When the Spirit wants to move a congregation in the direction of repentance and instead we do a song of rejoicing, we find ourselves in the undesirable position of opposing what God wants to do. Similarly if the Lord is speaking to us concerning his holiness what does it profit if we do a song of warfare? We are workers together with God (2 Cor. 6:1) and, as such, it behooves us to actually work together with him, not independently of him!

It is much easier to hear his heartbeat if we are close to him. We also need to have our fingers on the pulse of the local body we are ministering to. What are the needs of the body? Is there a particular season that the body is in? Jesus said that he only did what he saw the Father do (John 5:19). Having a sensitive spirit means paying attention to what the Father is doing and ministering in that direction.

This is not possible without spending time in prayer, developing relationships within the body and, most of all, having a genuine concern for those to whom you are ministering. When we are in tune with the Holy Spirit, we end up ministering directly to the needs of the body instead of using the shotgun approach, praying that we might partially hit the target.

There is also a musical side of sensitivity. As any student of music knows, there is more to good music than pitches and rhythms. Using the correct dynamics is very important to properly interpreting a song, and often that makes the difference between mediocrity and excellence. Dynamics simply means how you say what you say. You wouldn't run out of a building that is on fire and calmly whisper "fire". No, you would wave your arms and scream it out "**FIRE!!**"

The same applies to our praise and worship. When we do a song of joy, the music should invoke joy! A song about the awesomeness of God should sound awesome; an intimate song should sweep the hearer right into the throne room. It is both frustrating and ineffective when the lyrics and the music are saying two different things.

Many times musicians in a worship team underestimate the power of dynamics in music. Remember that fast is only fast because of slow. Loud is only loud because of soft. Many worship teams only have one volume level: loud! They start out loud and stay there. Within a song, and even within a set of songs, there should be a variety of dynamic levels. Attention to this one aspect of music will cause a band to sound much more mature in a small amount of time. And it will increase their ability to communicate what they sense the Lord is speaking.


**A spirit of integrity - a clear conscience before God and man**

We have already discussed the emphasis that God places on the heart when it comes to worship. A pure heart is always the priority issue with God. But when we speak of integrity we are dealing with not only the state of the heart, but with the outworking of that pure heart in a lifestyle of moral uprightness before God and man.

In 2 Corinthians Paul spends some time discussing how a minister of God should live. He calls those of us who are in the ministry to a high standard. He says that we are to be a fragrance of Jesus, that is, a tangible expression of the Son of God (2 Cor. 2:15). We must minister in sincerity, not using our position for our own profit (2 Cor. 2:17). We must renounce secret and shameful ways and any deception (2 Cor. 4:1-2). Here he is not talking merely about open and blatant sin, but being clean even in the secret places of our hearts. Of course we don't kill people or commit sexual sin or any other outward offense, but we are to also allow the Word of God to judge the thoughts and intents of our heart and put those wrong motives away from us as well. In fact, Paul says that we are to give no offense in any thing, so that the ministry will not be discredited (2 Cor. 6:3). No offense... in anything... those are all-inclusive words, but such is the standard we are called to.

Paul himself lived to this standard. When he stood before Felix he said "...I strive always to keep my conscience clear before God and man" (Acts 24:16). Amazingly, he was able to say things such as "Whatever you have learned or received or heard from, or seen in me, put into practice." (Phil. 4:9) and "... I urge you to imitate me." (1 Cor. 4:16). What an incredible thing to be able to say!

This is very important from the standpoint of ministry because no one can receive ministry from a person who has been discredited in their eyes. If our daily walk that others see is not upright in the eyes of God and man then our effectiveness is decreased or nullified altogether. If you think back perhaps you will agree that those who have ministered to you the most are those who have a sense of depth in their walk... a sort of profoundness and genuineness that comes from walking with God in integrity. Their life is not all surface. They have deep roots in God. They speak, not merely from *what they know*, but they impart *who they are*. The richness of that walk with God comes through. It is easy to receive from those people.

*No one can receive ministry from a person who has been discredited in their eyes... the gospel itself is discredited when it is proclaimed by a demon! The truth of the message does not negate the integrity of the messenger*

The fact that God is concerned with the integrity of his messengers is evident in the account of the demon possessed girl who followed Paul around crying "These man are the servants of the Most High God, who are telling you the way to be saved." (Acts 16:17). Was what she was saying not true? Does it not seem that by doing this she would be helping Paul and Silas to further the gospel? Then why did Paul turn around and rebuke her and cast the spirit out of her? Because the messenger is as important as the message. The gospel itself is discredited when it is proclaimed by a demon! The truth of the message does not negate the integrity of the messenger. In the same way, the validity of the songs we sing and the God we worship can be tainted by a walk that is less than upright. God give us hearts of integrity that Your glory may not be compromised!

**A spirit of consecration - poured out for Him**

To be consecrated is to be set apart for the service of God. It means we are different. It's not that we are better than anyone else, but that we are called to a different place of responsibility. A consecrated person orders his life around that thing he is consecrated to. The way he serves God orders the rest of his life and not the other way around.

Because we represent God, there are things that others may be able to do that we simply cannot do. If we are to fill our minds with God we must necessarily avoid filling them with things that are contrary to God and holy living. We must watch what our eyes see, our ears hear and our mouths speak. We must be good stewards of our time and monitor our walk before others.

Consecration is a sacrificing of ourselves. It is as though we are poured out for our Lord. And if we are to be poured out for the Lord, there is usually some form of ministry through which our devotion is expressed. But all of that ministry boils down, in the end, to people. Time after time God faithfully reminds me that it is people who are important. Not a job, a gift or an expression of ministry, but people. People are important to God. We cannot be consecrated to God without being consecrated to serving people.

In 2 Corinthians 4:10-12, Paul speaks to this pouring out of ourselves for others when he says "We always carry around in our body the death of Jesus, so that the life of Jesus may also be revealed in our body. For we who are alive are always being given over to death for Jesus' sake, so that his life may be revealed in our mortal body. So then death is at work in us, but life is at work in you." His attitude was, as he says in verse 15, all things are for the sake of those to whom he was ministering. There are many who are given to the work of God while neglecting the God of the work. God forbid that we be sold out to our expression of ministry and not to the God of the ministry and the people he loves.

The character quality that accompanies this spirit of consecration is faithfulness. Faithfulness can be defined as a continued, steadfast adherence to a person or thing to whom one is bound by an oath, duty, or obligation. It has to do with being trustworthy, loyal and dependable.

Proverbs 20:6 says that a faithful man is rare--a precious commodity. Consistency is a key to faithfulness. It is walking with God, that is, making decisions every day that are consistent with our commitment to God. Faithful men are the backbone to the church and the kingdom of God. It is to them that the truths of God are entrusted and by them those truths are passed on (2 Tim. 2:2). They were the heart of the work of the early church (1 Cor. 4:17; Eph. 6:21; Col. 4:7-9; 1 Peter 5:12; 1 Tim. 1:12)

God is our ultimate example of faithfulness. God's faithfulness toward us is tied to his love for us. In the same way, our love for him binds us to be faithful in our service to him. His great faithfulness is linked together with his mercies, which are new every morning! Even so each morning should bring a fresh consecrating of ourselves to Him.

# Levitical Worship
## Set Apart For His Service

Leading worship is a calling. A distinction must be made between those who simply have a gift to play or sing and those who are *worshipers*. Musicians are plentiful, but worshipers are few. Talent abounds but it is rare to find that talent consecrated and devoted solely to the service of the Savior. A true worshiper has set himself and his gift apart for the glory of God. They are often frustrated or feel unfulfilled and restless when they use their gift for any other purpose. They have a sense of calling on their lives that only finds contentment in the secret place of the Most High.

*Musicians are plentiful, worshipers are few.*

Perhaps the ministry of worship finds its closest parallel in the Old Testament ministry of the Levites. It was from among the Levites that skilled musicians were chosen to worship before the Lord in the tabernacle and temple. A study of these servants of the Lord will give us insight into the present day ministry of the worshiper.

**Levites choose the fear of the Lord**

The first mention of the Levites is in Exodus 32:26 when Moses looked upon the Israelites worshiping before the golden calf and said "Whoever is for the Lord, come to me." All the Levites rallied to him. They chose the Lord over the idolatry that their fellow Israelites were given to. A true worshiper will always be numbered on the Lord's side. His conscience will always draw him away from sin, no matter how many others are doing it. His heart calls Him back to fellowship with God. Keeping himself in a right relationship with God is priority in his life and even when he sins, he is quick to repent.

Hebrews 12:28 mentions two elements of acceptable worship: reverence and the fear of God. The fear of God is to hate all that is evil (Prov. 8:13). As we will see, the Levites were always conscientious in consecrating themselves to the Lord. So it is with the true worshiper. He loves what is right and hates sin because sin separates him from his God. When the call comes "Who is on the Lord's side?" he is first in line.

**Bearers of the Presence**

In Numbers 1:50-53 the Levites are appointed to be in charge of the tabernacle. They were to carry it, to take care of it and to camp around it. The tabernacle was the dwelling place of the ark of the covenant, or the abode of the presence of God. In the same way, true worshipers are to bear the presence of God (we are the temple of the Holy Spirit) and to camp around it, that is, to live in the presence of God.

Many people experience a type of culture shock when they come to a corporate praise meeting. They haven't spent any serious time in worship all week and when they encounter the presence of God in a meeting it takes them a while to recognize it and respond to it. It is as if they say, "This seems familiar...so this is what the presence of God feels like! Oh yes, I remember this from last week..." Usually it takes them until the end of the song service to enter into God's presence and then they have to sit down, never to sense the Spirit of God again until the next meeting.

Levites are not so. They long for the presence of God. They hang out with God all week. They are sensitive to Him and so they enter in quickly. They usually stand out in a crowd because they have that element of the presence of God stamped into their life. They are appointed to bear the presence of God and that is what they greatly desire. In fact Asaph, one of the chief Levitical musicians said in Psalm 73:26 that God was his portion, or his inheritance.

**Given to the Lord**

Numbers 3 tells us that the Levites were given to the Aaron the priest, to assist him and that they were *given to the Lord.* It is something quite special when God says, "They are mine". I am not implying that worship leaders enjoy a closer relationship to the Lord or that they are somehow given a privileged experience with God that is unattainable by other believers. I am, however, saying that those called as true worshipers have been set apart to be used in a special service unto the people, and unto the Lord.

*God wants us near. Jesus has made the way. But we cannot go there if we are not sprinkled and our conscience is not clean.*

The eighth chapter of Numbers gives us the consecration ceremony God prescribed for setting the Levites apart for His service. First God says to separate them from the others (verse 6). I believe it is important that we search out carefully those whom we believe God has placed His hand on as worshipers. *Not just anyone should be allowed to join a worship team.* Their call will be evident by a lifestyle and a sincere desire to worship God. They don't just love to sing, they love to commune with God and they are natural catalysts whose enthusiasm sparks worship in others. It is those whom we should separate from the other believers for the ministry of worship.

Secondly, the Levites were to be purified by the sprinkling of water (verse 7). The sprinkling of water in the New Testament has to do with the washing clean of our consciences before God so that we can draw near to God boldly, without fear. Many a worshiper has been beaten back from the presence of God by the Accuser of the brethren because his conscience was not clean before God. The blood of Jesus has made a way for all of our sins to be forgiven and cleansed, giving us a new position of purity and right standing before God. By appropriating that blood we can draw near to God in worship without fear of being rejected or chased away. God wants us near. Jesus has made the way. But we cannot go there if we are not sprinkled and our conscience is not clean.

The water also represents the washing of the water of the Word of God. As we will see later, knowing and being true to the Word of God is an essential element of our worship. In the next verse, even the clothes were washed, signifying the robes of righteousness which God has clothed us in.

After the separation and the cleansing, the Levites had to have their entire bodies shaved (verse 7). Without trying to over spiritualize, I suggest that this may have two meanings. First, it may denote transparency. We are told that everything is naked and open to the God whom we serve. I believe that God wants us to be open, sincere and 100% honest before Him and before people. That means being on the outside who we are on the inside. I also believe that the shaving of the flesh may refer to the putting away all filthiness of the flesh and spirit, and we are commanded to do in 2 Cor. 7:1. Removing sin from our lives is part of the process of consecrating ourselves to God's service.

**The seriousness of the call**

Finally, the Levites had hands laid on them and were given as an offering to the Lord as sacrifices were made to God (verses 8-19). This elaborate ceremony was what God required to set apart the Levites unto His service. It was a sober call to be a keeper of the presence, a servant in the house of God. It is no less serious today.

If we believe that we are called of God to a ministry of worship, then it naturally follows that we will stand before Him one day and give account to Him who judges righteously as to how we responded to that call. Faithfulness, diligence, excellence and integrity are necessary if we are to have anything to offer Him that will withstand the fiery trial.

**The tabernacle of David (1 Chron. 23-25)**

When David had the ark of the covenant brought to Jerusalem a new era began for the Levites. The Levite population grew until there were 24,000 who supervised the work of the Lord in the temple. Of those there were 4,000 whose only jobs, as recorded in scripture, were to praise the Lord with the musical instruments which David provided. 288 of those (the sons of Asaph, Heman and Jeduthun) were specially trained and were skillful in music for the Lord. It seems that the 288 were under the authority and instruction of their fathers and in turn were over the 4,000 other musicians.

As they submitted to the supervision of their God-given authorities, they flowed in their gifts, worshiped and prophesied on their instruments! The scripture is very clear that they were set apart for the ministry of prophesying as they played (or were accompanied by) different musical instruments.

Every team should have a recognized leader. The leader is the leader for a reason. Their gift has been recognized by the pastoral staff and the other team members are to submit to them. At the same time, they are under the authority of the pastors and elders of the church and should submit to them. This can be a problem if someone who has been a peer now becomes a leader. Sometimes their peers don't want to recognize their position of leadership. Pastors can help by validating and reinforcing their confidence in those chosen to lead. Sometimes a consecration ceremony where a laying on of hands "sets in" the new leader will greatly help the team leader to gain the respect he needs from the rest of the band. This kind of respect and unity was present in David's tabernacle and we need it as well today.


**The restoration of Davidic worship**
The wicked king Jereboam closed the temple and threw the Levites out of it because he had no use for them on account of his idolatries (2 Chron. 11:13-15). However, in 2 Chron. 29 we find that after the apostasy king Hezekiah cleansed and reopened the house of God and restored Levitical worship just as David had established it.

In this chapter we find that as the burnt offering was offered up, so was the offering of praise by the Levitical instrumentalists and the singers offered up. But as the people came forward to give their offerings to the priests to offer them up, it was quickly realized that there were too few priests to handle all of the offerings. Because of this the Levites helped the priests until the task was finished and until the other priests had been consecrated. FOR THE LEVITES HAD BEEN MORE CONSCIENTIOUS IN CONSECRATING THEMSELVES THAN EVEN THE PRIESTS HAD BEEN! (2 Chron. 29:34)

There is a very interesting parallel here. We should take our jobs as worshipers just as seriously as the pastors take their preaching and shepherding the flock. We should be just as prepared, just as clean, just as serious in our calling as they are in theirs. It's not a lesser job, just a different one. Ours is a very important job and we must treat it that way.


**Do not neglect your duty outside the "temple"**
Jesus, in His parable of the Good Samaritan, spoke of a particular Levite in a very non-flattering sense. As the man who was robbed and beaten lay helpless on the road, one of the men who passed him, looked at him, and walked around him, passing by on the other side of the road was a Levite.

Now it is certainly a bad enough that this man passed by someone in need. The fact that this man was a Levite - a worshiper, a temple keeper, perhaps even a musician or a singer - and that, chances are, he had just come from a time of worship in Jerusalem, fresh from the service of God, thinking he was right with God, and was on his way home when he stumbled into Jesus' story makes this a heavy indictment.

When we who are worshipers, who have been given so much, who love the presence of the Lord, can come out of the secret place and yet not walk out practical Christianity, something is dreadfully wrong.

By using this illustration Jesus was warning us that it is possible to think we are right with God and yet be disqualified by not doing something as simple as being a true neighbor. We must guard against that tendency to stay in the "temple" to the exclusion of the world which needs help. *"If anyone thinks he is something when he is nothing, he deceives himself." (Gal. 6:3)*

# Worship in the Life of David:
## A Secret Life With God

The man who penned the words "The Lord is my shepherd, I shall not want" had a rich and meaningful relationship with the God Whom he worshiped. This man after God's own heart bears studying in order to help us understand how to worship God as a way of life.

Admittedly, David had his faults. However, this man had an astounding consistency in worshiping God through every season and circumstance in His life. Let's take some time to consider David the worshiper.

**He worshiped in good times** - (2 Sam. 6:12-14; Ps.9)

David had many high points in his life: his triumph over Goliath, his anointings as king, his many victories in battle. However, if we could ask David what the single greatest moment of his life was he might well say it was when the Ark of the Covenant was brought to Jerusalem. He marked this occasion in his life by exuberant, extravagant and shameless worship.

In the highest points of his life David did not grow self-centered. He did not build a monument to himself, rather, he built an altar to God. He worshiped God with great enthusiasm. Unlike so many others who let their successes go to their head, David basically remained humble. David never took the glory for his victories, but acknowledged God.

**He worshiped in bad times** -- (Ps.3)

In the lowest points of his life, such as here, hiding in a cave from his enemies, David encouraged himself in the Lord. When his circumstances could have turned him bitter, he remembered the Lord's goodness.

I believe this Psalm is significant in that it shows us how to worship with our minds. *Self-control in our thought life is an integral part of our worship.* David spends the first part of the Psalm reflecting on how bad things were... and they really were bad. He was surrounded by those who had betrayed him in order to follow his erring son Absalom. The mocking of his enemies rang in his ear: "His God can never deliver him from our hands!" And they had almost persuaded him it was true. The word 'Selah' very likely means a musical interlude that causes one to pause and reflect on the lyrics of the song. *David was meditating on how bad his situation was!* If we could ask David what was the single worst time of his life, perhaps he would say it was here, hiding in the cave from his own son who had turned against him.

Then David changed his thoughts. His discipline in his thought life gained him new perspective and drove the fear from him. He began to meditate on the Lord and how He had protected and delivered him in the past. God had delivered him from the bear and the lion, as well as from the Philistine! He began to think about how God is his shield and he did not need to be afraid even of ten thousands of people who would set themselves against him... the Lord would arise and fight for him and shatter the teeth of the wicked!

*Self-control in our thought life is an integral part of our worship.*

Proverbs 25:28 says that a man who has no control over his spirit is like a city with no walls...completely open and accessible to the enemy. We are that way when we do not control our thoughts, opening the door to the devil to torment us and steal our worship. We are especially vulnerable to this in the low periods of our life. Yet, if we worship only in the good times, we really aren't worshiping. David had such an intense, life-encompassing love for God that it turned the tide and caused him to be an overwhelming conqueror, even in the worst times of his life.

There have been times when my wife and I, after dealing with the cares of the week, getting the children up early in order to get ready for the early worship service, getting there extra-early for a sound check and prayer, would have no mental unction to worship. In those times we fall back on the simple truth that "He is worthy to be worshiped." No matter how things are going, no matter how we feel at the moment, the one unchanging fact is that He is worthy. So we worship as an act of our will and God meets us and refreshes us. Remember the Psalmist said "I *will* enter His gates with thanksgiving..." Sometimes the "I will" is the essence of our worship.

**He worshiped while repenting and being chastened for his sin** -- (2 Sam. 12:15-23; Ps.51)

Even in his remorse over his sin, David drew near to God and didn't run away. His overwhelming passion was to be clean and close to God again. Repentance is turning from sin and turning to God. Repentance is a positive thing, not a negative thing. It is a lifestyle, not an event.

The episode of the sickness and death of David and Bathsheba's child (2 Sam. 12) shows David's great insight to the merciful nature of God. Why would he fast and pray for the life of a child that God had already said would surely die? David himself gives the answer in verse 22-23 -- "I thought, 'Who knows? The Lord may be gracious to me and let the child live....'" When most of us would have shunned the presence of God because of our guilt, David approached the throne of God boldly with a petition.

David knew enough of what he called the Lord's "lovingkindnesses and tendermercies" to offer his petition even when judgment was passed. And then, when the child died, he arose, washed himself, changed his clothes, went to the house of the Lord and, can you imagine, worshiped. Even though his sin was grievous, his punishment devastating and his prayer unanswered, David knew God was just and true in all His dealings. He accepted the judgment of the Lord and worshiped.

**He worshiped when facing fear and danger** -- (Ps. 56:3)

The wonderful thing about the account that God gives about the life of David is that it is brutally honest. David, while portrayed as a hero of the faith, is also portrayed as totally human. No pains were taken to hide his mortal side. Along side the passion, the courage, the faith, the steadfastness, the purity and the zeal for God are the times in his life when he was afraid, irrational, angry, weak, given to vice and disobedient.

There is an old proverb that says "When you kick a bucket, what is inside comes out." Adversity has a way of revealing exactly what is in our hearts. What comes out when your bucket is kicked?

What did David do when facing danger or fear? He worshiped: "When I am afraid I will trust in you."


**He worshiped in the way he sought God's will and direction for his life –**
(2 Sam. 2:1)

Oftentimes the most faith trying times in our lives come when we can't seem to get clear direction for our lives. We inquire of the Lord, but don't always hear right away. How we respond in times like these reflects our heart concerning God's character, his sovereignty, his goodness and our fear of the Lord. Will we rush on ahead with plans of our own making or will we patiently wait on the Lord?

Unlike Saul, who made rash decisions and did not wait on the Lord, David often sought the Lord intensely and thoroughly and waited until he got an answer before he moved. This is a subtle, but no less important manifestation of an attitude of worship. Submitting the seasons of our lives to the will of God is a true mark of worship.


**He worshiped in seeing that promotion comes from the Lord** -- (2 Sam. 5:1-12)

He did not think that the strength of his own hand had gotten him where he was. David knew that it was the Lord who had established him as king over Israel. As worship leaders we are in a particularly precarious place. When we hold a position or walk in a gifting it is so easy to steal the glory from God. It is so easy to say "my strength has gotten me to this place."

In Exodus 13 we see God establishing the dedication of the firstborn to Himself. He was emphatic about the reason for this: that they would know that "the *Lord* brought you out of Egypt with *his* mighty hand". He said this over and over in that chapter. It was essential that the Israelites knew that it was not the power of their own hand that got them where they were. It was not by might, nor power, but by the Spirit of God.

So it is with us. Part of our worship is realizing that promotion comes from the Lord. "For *from* him and *through* him and *to* him are all things. To him be the glory forever! Amen" (Romans 11:36). Our times are in His hands.


**He worshiped by having a great passion for the presence of the Lord –**
(2 Samuel 6)

David had an amazing revelation of the presence of God. He was way ahead of his time in his understanding of the heart of God to be with his people. I see David's perception of God as he relates to his people to be a fulcrum between the Old Covenant and the New Covenant. He understood that God was awesome and holy, and yet he felt that God did not want to be shut up in a box or hidden behind a veil.

David longed for the presence of God so much that he started a great campaign to bring the Ark of the Covenant to Jerusalem. He pitched a tent in his back yard and put the Ark there, near him, where he could worship often. No wonder he wrote such things as "you will fill me with joy in your presence, with eternal pleasures at your right hand" (Ps. 16:11). And when he sinned his great concern was "Do not cast me from your presence or take your Holy Spirit from me" (Ps. 51:11)

His great desire to be close to the Lord is evident in that unlike other kings who pledged allegiance to Jehovah and then forsook him, David never became an idolater.

### He worshiped in that he had an excellent spirit

Whatever David did, he did well. In the season of his life when he was a shepherd, he protected the flock even with his life (1 Sam 17:34-36). As a worshiper, he gave himself whole-heartedly, setting up a system of constant worship (1 Chron. 15:1-29) and personally going all out in his worship of God even before the eyes of men (2 Samuel 6:14-23). As a warrior, he conquered what he believed God had given into his hand (2 Sam. 5:6-7).

*David, as a rule, was not a mediocre man. He had a spirit of excellence about, him. It was as though doing a thing with all his might was a part of his service or worship to God.*

As a musician he was said to be "cunning" or "skillful" on his instrument (1 Samuel 16:18). This verse also says that David was mighty, valiant, wise, and the Lord was with him! David, as a rule, was not a mediocre man. He had a spirit of excellence, of quality about him. It was as though doing a thing with all his might was a part of his service or worship to God.

### Most of all, David worshiped by having a secret life with God

Reactions like this don't just happen. They are built into a life over a period of years by having a secret life with God. David's relationship with God was not only public (as a Pharisee's was) but it was mostly private. What was built into him through the private times came out during the crucial times of his life.

In the scripture in 1 Samuel 16, Saul's men had obviously seen David play his instrument, but where? It had to be in the fields as David was tending the sheep and worshiping the Lord. Honestly, when was the last time someone walked in and found you worshiping alone? Or praying alone? David had a secret life with God, and it was out of that secret life with God that he was called to higher things in God's plan for him.

No one is suddenly different from his habits. David didn't just become an upright man whom the Lord was with. His life, habits and customs were forged out of his personal walk with God. We are in public what we become in private before the Lord.

God records for us the lives of Saul and David and we find a multitude of similarities between the two men. Their background was identical in many ways, and yet their lives ended completely opposite from one another. How could this be? Modern psychology tells us that like circumstances yield like results: not so in the kingdom of God. David's life was blessed and Saul's was cursed because of one important difference: David had a secret life with God while Saul did not. David's passion for God was not just show. It was genuine and it spilled over into every aspect of his life. This is the essence of Romans 12:1:

*"Therefore, I urge you, brothers, in view of God's mercy, to offer your bodies as living sacrifices, holy and pleasing to God -- this is your spiritual act of worship."*

# The Tabernacle of David, the Tabernacle of God

For many years there has been teaching on the rebuilding of the tabernacle of David. There have been many interpretations as to what this foretold restoration is to be and what it means practically in the life and practice of the Church. The scripture that this teaching is based on is Acts 15:16-17:

*After this I will return and build again the tabernacle of David, which is fallen down; and I will build again the ruin thereof, and I will set it up;*

*That the residue of men might seek after the Lord, and all the Gentiles, upon whom my name is called, saith the Lord, who doeth all these things."*

Whatever else this passage might imply, the context certainly speaks of two things: 1) the house of David (which seems to mean the system of worship set up by David) will be reestablished by the Lord Himself and, 2) the reestablishing of it will result in the Gentiles coming to Christ as never before.

There has been much teaching on this concept, some of which holds to the belief that the literal system of worship established by David (2 Chronicles 23-25) where skillful musicians, appointed and consecrated for the purpose of praising God twenty-four hours a day, will be set up once again in the Church. There are city-wide movements in our day where this very thing is happening.

This is a wonderful thing and much good will come to the kingdom of God on earth through this type of worship/intercession, but I believe it is not only the literal aspects, but the very heart of this tabernacle of David that God wants to restore. And when He does restore it, what will follow is an outpouring of salvation as those who do not know the Lord come to know Him through this rebirth of worship.

In studying the tabernacle of David, I have come to believe that it is actually modeled on the "tabernacle of God" as seen in Revelation chapters 4 and 5 and described in Revelation 21:3-5:

*"And I heard a great voice out of heaven saying, behold, the tabernacle of God is with men, and he will dwell with them, and they shall be his people, and God himself shall be with them, and be their God.*

*And God shall wipe away all tears from their eyes, and there shall be no more death, neither sorrow, nor crying, neither shall there be any more pain" for the former things are passed away.*

*And he that sat upon the throne said, Behold, I make all things new..."*

As we study this tabernacle of God and the historical tabernacle of David, we can see that together they present to us the heart of what God wants to restore. The Lamb is the instrument of this reconciliation and restoration... that is why He is worthy!

# God's restored tabernacle is:

### 1) Characterized by the presence of God

As we read in Revelation 21:3, the tabernacle of God is *"with men"*. It has always been God's heart to be with men. From the walks with Adam and Eve in the cool of the day in the garden to the incarnation of Christ to this splendid scene when God declares that His final dwelling place is to be with the redeemed of all the ages, God has always wanted to be *with men*.

David himself pitched a tent for the Ark in his own back yard. What a revelation of the presence of God he had! Indeed, his prayer in Psalm 51 was *"Do not cast me from your presence or take your Holy Spirit from me."* David had witnessed the state of Saul when the presence of God had departed from him. David did not want that to happen to him (1 Samuel 16:14).

The powerful, manifest presence of God is a life-changing force. When you are in His presence, you worship. A man in the presence of God is a man confronted with his sin before a holy God. It is no wonder that Gentiles will come to the Lord as His presence is restored in an increasingly powerful way in His Church.

### 2) Throne-focused

*"At once I was in the Spirit, and there before me was a throne in heaven with someone sitting on it. And the one who sat there had an appearance of jasper and carnelian, A rainbow, resembling an emerald, encircled the throne. Surrounding the throne were twenty-four other thrones, and seated on them were twenty-four elders. They were dressed in white and had crowns of gold on their heads. From the throne came flashings of lightning, rumblings and peals of thunder. Before the throne seven lamps were blazing. These are the seven spirits of God. Also before the throne was what looked like a sea of glass, clear as crystal.*

*In the center, around the throne, were four living creatures, and they were covered with eyes, in front and in back...Day and night they never stopped saying: "Holy, holy, holy is the Lord God Almighty, who was, and is, and is to come."*

*Whenever the living creatures give glory, honor and thanks to him who sits on the throne and who lives for ever and ever, the twenty-four elders fall down before him who sits on the throne, and worship him who lives for ever and ever. They lay their crowns before the throne and say: "You are worthy, our Lord and God, to receive glory and honor and power, for you created all things, and by your will they were created and have their being.""* Revelation 4:2-6, 8-11

*"Then I saw a Lamb, looking as if it had been slain, standing **in the center of the throne**, encircled by the four living creatures and elders."*
Revelation 5:6 (Emphasis added)

What images come to mind when you think of the word throne? Sovereignty, authority, power, rule, kingship, supremacy, government, dominion.

The implication of this scripture is obvious: the Lamb has supreme and final authority in heaven and on earth. He has absolute sway over all mankind and every created being. In the tabernacle of God, Jesus rules!

Is this not a major theme in the tabernacle of David?

*"The Lord is King forever and ever..."* Psalm 10:16

*"Lift up your heads, O you gates, be lifted up you ancient doors, that the King of glory may come in. Who is this king of glory? The Lord strong and mighty, the Lord mighty in battle."* Psalm 25:7-8

*"...the Lord is enthroned as King forever."* Psalm 29:10

*"For God is the King of all the earth; sing to him a psalm of praise."* Psalm 47:7

*"The Lord reigns, let the earth be glad..."* Psalm 97:1

David, the king, knew that there was a King of kings and that homage to Him was non-negotiable. When you truly see the One seated on the throne and the rank and authority that goes with that position, you have no choice but to bow in worship. Jesus must reign supreme in our worship. We must not presume to wear a crown when all of heaven casts theirs down before Him. No flesh will glory in His presence. His kingship must be the focus of our worship.

### 3) Lamb-centered

*Then I saw a Lamb, looking as if it has been slain, standing in the center of the throne, encircled by the four living creatures and the elders... he came and took the scroll from the right hand of him who sat on the throne. And when he had taken it, the four living creatures and the twenty-four elders fell down before the Lamb... And they sang a new song:*

*"You are worthy to take the scroll and open its seals, because you were slain, and with your blood you purchased men for God from every tribe and language and people and nation. You have made them to be a kingdom and priests to serve our God, and they will reign on the earth. "*

*Then I looked and heard the voice of many angels, numbering thousands upon thousands and ten thousand times ten thousand. They encircled the throne and the living creatures and the elders. In a loud voice they sang:*

*"Worthy is the Lamb who was slain, to receive power and wealth and wisdom and strength and honor and glory and praise!" Then I heard every creature in heaven and on earth and under the earth and on the sea, and all that is in them, singing:*

*"To him who sits on the throne and to the Lamb be praise and honor and glory and power forever and ever!" The four living creatures said "Amen." And the elders fell down and worshiped."* Revelation 5:6-14

Heaven's worship is centered around the Jesus, the Lamb. He is in the midst of the throne, in the midst of the creatures, in the midst of the elders, in the midst of the throng of angels and He is the focus and the object of the praise of all those in heaven, on earth, under the earth and in the sea.

*God desires to rebuild His tabernacle of praise where the content of our worship is the message of the cross and the Lamb takes His rightful place "in the midst" of our worship.*

The reasons are simple. Number one, He is worthy. Because of who He is and what He has done, he deserves our everlasting praise. But also, when you see such love as He gave in buying our fallen souls back to God, you can't help but worship.

David and the psalmists of his day tapped in prophetically to this message of the Messiah who would redeem all mankind. Out of David's tabernacle came over 20 Messianic psalms that in some way foretell Jesus' coming, his death or his resurrection.

God desires to rebuild His tabernacle of praise where the content of our worship is the message of the cross and the Lamb takes his rightful place "in the midst" of our worship.

Several years ago a precious old saint in our fellowship named brother Harold, nearly eighty years old, came up to me after a worship service, took my hand and gently but firmly said "I just wanted you to know that we sang for twenty-five minutes this morning before we ever mentioned the name of Jesus… just wanted you to know."

I have never been so rightly rebuked. That was a time of refreshing and restoration of worship on the church in general. We sang about warfare, about praise, about shouting and dancing, about singing…about everything but Jesus! By God's grace I have determined in my heart to never have it said of our worship that we went even a portion of a service without making Jesus central and supreme. That doesn't mean we never sing a song that doesn't use the word Jesus in the lyrics, but that we are characterized by keeping Jesus in His place of prominence. The Lamb of God must be the center of our church's worship.

**4) Extravagant Worship**

In the restored tabernacle of David there will be no half-hearted worship. In the passage quoted above you see that the worship in heaven is extravagant. Like Mary, who poured costly perfume on Jesus' feet without consideration of what it cost her, we will lavish the Son of God with our uninhibited praise.

Imagine a throne surrounded by an emerald rainbow, twenty-four thrones and elders, crowns, blazing lamps, a crystal sea, extraordinary creatures, angels and throngs of people all singing with loud voices to the Lamb. That is extravagant!

David's tabernacle had 24,000 Levites, 4,000 of whom were musicians, divided up into 24 courses and worshipping 24 hours a day. That is extravagant.

I think of Solomon on the day he dedicated the temple of the Lord: he offered twenty-two thousand cattle and one hundred and twenty thousand sheep and goats! (1 Kings 8:63) Now *that* is extravagant! Perhaps God desires to increase our vision and the scope of our worship so that we do it with our whole heart unto Him!

The last three characteristics of the tabernacle of God seem to be inseparably bound together in the expression of praise that went on in David's tabernacle and that goes on in heaven. I will briefly list them and then talk about the use of them together.

### 5) Musical

In Revelation 5:8 we see that the living creatures and the elders each have a harp with which they evidently accompanied themselves as they sang a new song (vss. 9-10, 12, 13).

We also see in 1 Chronicles 25:1-6 that harps, lyres and cymbals were used in the ministry in the tabernacle of David. In Psalm 150 all groups of instruments are listed: winds, brass, strings and percussion. I believe that if David were alive today he would say "Praise Him on the synthesizers and sequencers!"

### 6) Intercessory

Again, in Revelation 5:8 we see that the living creatures and the elders were holding golden bowls full of the prayers of Gods saints. The psalms are often prayers for deliverance, mercy, judgement, etc. A powerful spirit of intercession flows out of this worship that God wants to restore in our day.

> *...music, prayer and prophecy flow together as one to enhance God's purpose in our worship. Anointed worship music releases a spirit of intercession and an atmosphere for the prophetic voice of God to come forth.*

### 7) Prophetic

In Revelation 5:9 we are told that the living creatures and the elders sang a "new song". Not only was it a song that had never been sung before, but it was a prophetic declaration of the power, scope and magnitude of the blood of the Lamb. This prophetic song sparked other spontaneous new songs from the angels (verse 12) and all creatures in heaven, on earth, under the earth and on the sea (verse 13).

Back in 1 Chronicles 25:1, the sons of Asaph, Heman and Jeduthun prophesied on their instruments. So we also see that a prophetic anointing is released through this powerful worship.

It is crucial that we who minister in the realm of worship understand that music, prayer and prophecy flow together as one to enhance God's purpose in our worship.

Anointed worship music releases a spirit of intercession and an atmosphere for the prophetic voice of God to come forth.

Be sensitive during your times of worship of this prompting of the Holy Spirit to pray. Breathe your songs out as prayers to the Lord. Pray for His kingdom to come, for His will to be done. Pray for His mercy, His compassion and healing. Pray for His deliverance from evil. Pray for Him to stretch out His hand and do wonders again. Release your prayers to Him in song and watch Him answer!

Also be aware of prophetic inspiration as you worship. God wants to speak to us and through us as we worship. He is not silent but we must listen and be obedient to speak or sing His word. Perhaps you might look over the sections on *"Spirit of sensitivity – having ears to hear"* and *"God speaks to us – releasing the prophetic anointing"* as well as *"Practical tips for prophetic worship"* for more study on these topics.

It seems that all of these elements were present in the Tabernacle of David, which God told us He will restore, as well as the 'Tabernacle of God" which is to dwell among men. Let's make it our prayer that God will give us His grace to incorporate them into the fabric of our worship times.

# Priming Your Praise Pump

Many people fail to experience the fullness of worship as God intended because they fail to prepare a sacrifice. In the Old Testament, a person *never* came to worship without bringing something. They brought a pure offering, the one prescribed for the specific type of worship and the best they could afford and they came to the priests to offer it up to the Lord.

David said at one time "I will not offer up to the Lord something which cost me nothing". How different this is from the man today who rarely thinks about God throughout the week, stays up late on the night before the service, gets up late, runs through the shower, drives slightly over the speed limit on the way to church, spilling his coffee, in order to make it on time, slides in the back door of the church just in time to hear the last chorus of the last song and wonders why he didn't get anything out of worship (never contemplating the fact that God never got anything from him).

*Satan fell by stealing the worship that rightfully and exclusively belonged to God and he has been stealing worship ever since.*

**Satan, thief of worship**
Many theologians agree that whatever job Lucifer had before he fell through pride, one thing seems clear: he held the exalted position of a heavenly creature covering the throne of God and seemed to be greatly involved in the trafficking of the praise of all creation to the very throne of God. If this was true then a very important and ironic thing happened when he decided to exalt himself above the throne of God (see Ezekiel 28:11-19 and Isaiah 14:12-17). His entire job was to give glory to God and yet he began to covet some of that glory for himself. He who was a channel of praise to God decided to steal some of that praise for himself. The chief of worshipers became the chief of demons.

Satan fell by stealing the worship that rightfully and exclusively belonged to God and he has been stealing worship ever since. I believe that there are many ways in which he steals our worship from God: The idolatry which comes through the lust of the eyes, the lust of the flesh and the pride of life; the distractions caused by the cares of the world which fill our thoughts; the constant busy-ness that consumes our time and robs us of fellowship with God; the guilty feelings caused by unconfessed sin; his constant accusations by which he accuses us to God. All of these and many more he throws at us in order to steal our worship from God.

I believe that there are specific steps we can take which will thwart Satan's purposes and preserve our praise for God, to Whom it rightfully belongs. This acrostic will help assure that our praise pump is primed and ready at all times.

P = **Prepare**
R = **Repent**
I = **Invest**
M = **Minister to the Lord**
E = **Enter in Quickly**

## **P**repare – *"...prepare your hearts unto the Lord, to serve him only"* (1 Sam. 7:3)

All week long, stay in an attitude of worship. Be sensitive to the mind of the Lord. Let the Word of Christ dwell in you richly, and pray. Come to the service with an idea of what God is speaking. Get plenty of rest so that you are prepared physically. Listen to praise music all week long. Get up early enough that you don't have to rush.

Preparing prevents Sunday morning "culture shock" from stealing your worship. Perhaps you have experienced this phenomenon. You are in a worship service and your mind is preoccupied with a host of things, as it has been all week. Three-quarters way through the service you finally begin to focus on the Lord. Preparing can help you in the discipline of setting aside the cares of the world in order to truly worship.

## **R**epent – *"Having therefore, brethren, boldness to enter into the holiest by the blood of Jesus..."* (Heb. 10:19-22)

Many are hindered from the presence of God by a guilty conscience. Make every effort to walk in the light, but if you sin, deal with it quickly. Repent and restore your fellowship with God and with your brother. Know that when we confess our sin, He is faithful and just to forgive us our sins and cleanse us from all unrighteousness (1 John 1:9)

Repenting prevents accusations from the enemy from stealing and hindering your worship. Satan whispers his lies, accusing us before God, accusing God to us, and accusing us to ourselves. But thanks be to God, the blood of Jesus speaks louder than those accusations! Jesus died to bring us to fellowship with God. Enjoy His provision!

## **I**nvest – *"I will not offer to the Lord that which costs me nothing."* (2 Sam. 24:24)

You can invest in the service by spending time praying for God's kingdom to come and His will to be done, practicing your vocals or your instrument, by giving of yourself to serve the body of believers to whom you are ministering and by spending time in God's presence and His Word. When you do this you are eager to see a payoff in that investment. What joy and fulfillment you experience when God brings His kingdom and His presence in the services.

Investing prevents apathy and laziness from stealing your worship. Living a lifestyle of worship is a diligent task. The half-hearted don't make it. God tells us to do everything our hand finds to do with all of our might. There is no place for indifference in this calling.

## Ministering to God – *"My eyes are ever toward the Lord..."* (Ps. 25:15)

The first song in the Bible (Exodus 15) begins this way: "I will sing *unto the Lord*." This is a key to the worship leader's worship. We must fix our eyes on Jesus and sing to Him, not to the congregation. Our focus is not on people, it is on God.

The worship leader's job is to *lead worship* (what a revelation). Let me say it another way-- leading worship involves two things: worshiping and leading. Leading does not mean pointing, it means going there and letting others follow you. For example, if you wanted to come to my house, I could say "Go to this road, turn right and then take a left...etc." Would I be leading you? No, I would be giving you directions. If I said "Get in your car and follow me, I'll take you there", then I am leading. It is the same in leading worship. I don't point to God and say "There He is, go ahead...worship Him!" Instead, I worship Him and allow you to follow me into His presence. *That* is leading.

We cannot lead where we are not first going. Our job is to work ourselves out of a job. By that I mean we are not constantly trying to convince the people to worship. There are few things more annoying to me than a worship leader who constantly preaches at the people. That person is cheerleading, not leading worship. We are to instigate worship, strike the match and light the fuse. Then we are to step back and worship and let the people worship. Perhaps we would be more correct in our thinking if we saw ourselves as "lead worshipers" instead of "worship leaders".

Focusing on Jesus and ministering to Him prevents distractions in the service itself from keeping our attention away from the One who is worthy of our worship.

## Enter in quickly – *"Whatever you do, do it with all your heart as unto the Lord."* (Col. 3:23)

Right from the first song, set your mind on the Lord and worship Him. There is a Latin phrase that has become rather popular recently: *Carpe diem* -- it means "seize the day". In other words, wherever you are, be *all* there. Drink in the moment and live it to the fullest. That is a great idea, but unfortunately not too many people live there. Don't waste any time going through the motions. *Really* worship God, right from the start.

Entering in quickly prevents your mind from wondering and sets you in a place to hear the voice of the Spirit of God early in the service.

I challenge you to consciously practice these suggestions for "priming your praise pump" for 6 weeks and see what happens. It might just revolutionize your personal worship experience, not to mention your congregations'!

# Worship and the Heart

Of all of the major references to music or worship in the Bible, I don't know of one that doesn't include the condition of the heart of man before God. God is primarily concerned about the heart. Jesus said to the Pharisees, *"You hypocrites, Isaiah was right when he prophesied about you, 'These people honor me with their lips, but their heart is far from me. They worship me in vain; their teachings are but rules taught by men."* (Matt. 15:7-9) If our hearts are not right, our worship is vain and repulsive to God. Review these scriptures which we have discussed before:

> John 4 -- The woman at the well asked Jesus questions about the outward aspects of worship while Jesus pointed out her sinful condition and showed her that true worship comes out of the heart.

> Amos 5 -- God says He hates our worship and He will not hear the noise of our songs because our hearts are not right with Him. We mustn't just sing songs, but we must let justice flow like rivers.

> 1 Samuel 16:14-23 -- David was a man whose heart was right with the Lord and therefore God used him to play his instrument and chase demons away.

> Col. 3:16 -- Letting the word of the Lord dwell in us richly is a prerequisite to singing psalms, hymns and spiritual songs.

> Eph. 5:18-19 -- Being filled with the Holy Spirit is a prerequisite to singing psalms, hymns and spiritual songs.

> Heb. 10:22 -- We draw near to God with pure hearts, cleansed from an evil conscience.

> Psalm 24:3-5 -- Who will ascend to God's holy mountain and abide in His presence? He who has clean hands and a pure heart.

> Romans 12:1-2 -- Our reasonable form of spiritual worship is presenting our bodies to God as a living sacrifice, holy and acceptable, not being conformed to this world, but transformed by the renewing of our mind.

> 2 Chron. 5:11-14 -- When all of the priests were sanctified, the glory of the Lord fell and the house of the Lord was filled with a cloud, the manifest presence of God, so that the priests could not even stand to minister.

> 2 Chron. 20:1-30 -- Jehoshaphat and the people of Judah were humble before the Lord in fasting and prayer. They were in a position to hear the voice of the Lord.

Jehoshaphat had brought the people back to the Lord, appointed righteous judges, and commanded the Levites to do their job with a perfect heart (chapter 19). That is why when they sent the singers first in the battle, the enemy was routed.

> Psalm 51 -- The Lord does not delight in sacrifices or burnt offerings but the sacrifices of God are a broken and humble spirit.

*The following is an outline of what I go over with every worship team I work with. If you don't have a vision, you perish. These guidelines (along with others the Lord may give you as you seek Him) will help you to have a unity in direction and purpose as a team. It is a good idea to review these points periodically.*

# Our Worship Team Vision

Each one of us is here because we believe that God has called us into this ministry. If He has called us, there are responsibilities that go along with the call. We will stand before God and give account to Him of how we have used the gifts He has given us. To whom much is given, much is required. Here are the core values we must have to go where God wants us to go as worshipers:

## 1) Live the Life -

> We must maintain the integrity of our relationship with God. Honesty, transparency, freedom from sin and the fear of the Lord must be what we are characterized by. Our calling requires us to be "examples of the believer, in word, in conversation, in charity, in spirit, in faith, in purity." (1 Tim. 4:12) We can never stop stressing the importance of integrity because God never stops stressing it.

> We must be worshipers all week long. Develop a lifestyle of worship: practice the presence of the Lord; cultivate a thankful heart and a beautiful relationship with the Father; take "praise vacations" throughout the day.

## 2) Commitment

> <u>To the body</u> -- We are not set up front to look pretty or to play pretty. We are called to *serve* the body. We must commit to pray for them, practically minister to them in other ways beside worship and establish relationships. God pours out His blessing where there is unity. This is why we require you to be a member of the church in order to minister to the body.

> <u>To the band</u> -- Grow in fellowship with your band members. Homogenize -- become a tight group both spiritually and musically. Have a specific time of ministry to each other during practices.

> <u>To increasing your ability</u> -- Growing in general skills is the key to liberty in worship. Vocal control and technique, understanding of harmony and elementary music theory, growing in technique on your instrument, practicing during the week, critical listening to good players and singers, memorization of material all brings freedom, clarity expression and depth to our worship.

## Concerning Practices

> Practice is mandatory -- If you don't practice, you don't play. Whatever time your band decides to practice, as well as pre-service practices and prayer, except for emergencies and special pre-arranged occasions, you need to be there.

> The principle of authority -- Each team has a leader. The leader is the *leader* and there is a reason why *he/she* is the leader. There is a recognized call of God on their life to function in this capacity. Listen to him/her. Do all you can to make the practices go smoothly. Do not waste time by playing independently while the leader is talking. Constructive criticism is healthy so receive it. Do not wear your heart on your sleeve if your ideas of how things should go are not accepted by the leader. Bad attitudes and pride grieve the Holy Spirit.

> A time for prayer and bonding -- We want to establish a time of prayer at each practice to pray for each other, for the body and that the band and the congregation will come to the service primed! Pray for God to be free to bring His kingdom and to do as He wishes during our services.

> Growing musically -- Use practice to get familiar with the music so that you don't have to be tied down to it during the services.

> Work on group dynamics -- not just intros, modulations and outros, but loud and soft, fast and slow...learn to really communicate with your music.

> Don't forget to worship -- What a novel idea! Practice isn't entirely mechanical. Actually worship and love on the Lord during practice. Take time to play in the spirit, sing new songs to the Lord, listen for the prophetic voice of the Lord. Practice chord progressions to sing in the spirit with.

# Why We Worship The Way We Do
(What God says about how we should worship Him)
or
# Worship is a verb!

**Singing** (over 120 references)
Psalm 30:4 – *"Sing to the Lord you saints of His; praise His holy name."*

Psalm 95:1 – *"Come let us sing for joy to the Lord; let us shout aloud to the Rock of our salvation."*

Psalm 47:6 – *"Sing praises to God, sing praises; Sing praises to our King, sing praises."*

Psalm 27:6 – *"…I will sing and make music to the Lord."*

Ephesians 5:19 – *"Speak to one another with psalms, hymns and spiritual songs. Sing and make music in your heart to the Lord."*

Colossians 3:16 -- *"Let the word of Christ dwell in you richly as you teach and admonish one another with all wisdom and as you sing psalms hymns and spiritual songs with songs of gratitude in your heart to God."*

**Clapping**
Psalm 47:1 – *"Clap your hands, all you nations; shout to God with cries of joy."*

**Dancing**
Psalm 149:3 – *"Let them praise His name with dancing."*

Psalm 150:4 – *"Praise Him with tambourine and dancing."*

2 Samuel 6:14-15 – *"David, wearing a linen ephod, danced before the Lord with all his might, while he and the entire house of Israel brought up the ark of the Lord with shouts and the sound of trumpets."*

Exodus 15:20 – *"Then Miriam the prophetess, Aaron's sister, took a tambourine in her hand, and all the women followed her, with tambourines and dancing."*

**"Rejoice" literally means "to spin, spring, leap, jump for joy, skip"

## Lifting Hands
Psalm 134:2 – *"Lift up your hands in the sanctuary and praise the Lord."*

Psalm 63:4 – *I will praise You as long as I live, and in Your name I will lift up my hands."*

Lamentations 3:41 – *" Let us lift up our hearts and our hands to God in heaven…"*

Psalm 143:6 – *"I spread out my hands to you; my soul thirsts for You like a parched land."*

1 Timothy 2:8 – *" I want men everywhere to lift up holy hands in prayer, without anger or disputing."*


## Shouting
Psalm 47:1 – *"…shout to God with cries of joy."*

Psalm 27:6 – *"…at His tabernacle I will sacrifice with shouts of joy"*

Psalm 98:4 – *"Shout for joy to the Lord all the earth, burst into jubilant song with music."*


## Standing
Deuteronomy 10:8 – *"At that time the Lord set apart the tribe of Levi to carry the ark of the covenant of the Lord, to stand before the Lord to minister and to pronounce blessings in His name, as they still do today."*


## Kneeling/Bowing
Psalm 95:6 – *"Come, let us bow down in worship, let us kneel before the Lord our maker."*

Ephesians 3:14 – *"For this reason I kneel before the Father, from Whom the whole family in heaven and on earth derives it's name."*


## Singing a new song
Psalm 149:1 – *"Sing to the Lord a new song."*

Ps. 40:3 – *"He put a new song in my mouth, a hymn of praise to our God."*

Psalm 98:1 – *"Sing to the Lord a new song, for He has done marvelous things…"*

Psalm 144:9 – *I will sing a new song to you , O God…"*

Revelation 5:9 – *"And they sang a new song: "You are worthy to take the scroll and open its seals…"*

Revelation 14:3 – *"And they sang a new song before the throne…"*

## Laughter
Psalm 126:2-3 – *"Our mouths were filled with laughter, our tongues with songs of joy…the Lord has done great things for us, and we are filled with joy."*

## Loud Noise/Loud Voice
2 Chronicles 20:19 – *Then some of the Levites… stood up and praised the Lord, the God of Israel, with a very loud voice."*

Psalm 81:1 – *"Sing for joy to God our strength; shout aloud to the God of Jacob!"*

Luke 17:15 – *"One of them, when he saw he was healed, came back, praising God in a loud voice."*

Luke 19:37 – *"…the whole crowd of disciples began joyfully to praise God in loud voices for all the miracles they have seen."*

Revelation 7:10 – *"And they cried out in a loud voice: 'Salvation belongs to our God, who sits on the throne, and unto the Lamb.'"*

## With Musical Instruments
Psalm 150:3-6 – *"Praise Him with the sounding of the trumpet, praise Him with the harp and the lyre, praise Him with tambourine and dancing, praise Him with the strings and flute, praise Him with the clash of cymbals, praise Him with resounding cymbals."*
\*\* Note that all of the classifications of instruments are included: Wind, brass, string, percussion.

Revelation 5:8 – *"And when he had taken it, the four living creatures and the twenty-four elders fell down before the Lamb. Each one had a harp…"*

## Banners
Psalm 20:5 – *"We will shout for joy when you are victorious and will lift up our banners in the name of our God."*

## Singing in the Spirit (tongues)
1 Corinthians 14:14-15 – *"For if I pray in a tongue, my spirit prays, but my mind is unfruitful. So what shall I do? I will pray with my spirit, but I will also pray with my mind; I will sing with my spirit, but I will also sing with my mind."*

## Prophecy
1 Chronicles 25:1 – *"David, together with the commanders of the army, set apart some of the sons of Asaph, Heman and Jeduthun for the ministry of prophesying, accompanied by harps, lyres and cymbals…"*

1 Corinthians 14:1-4,31 – *"Follow the way of love and eagerly desire the spiritual gifts, especially the gift of prophecy. For anyone who speaks in a tongue does not speak to men but to God. Indeed, no one understands him, he utters mysteries with his spirit. But everyone who prophesies speaks to men for their strengthening, encouragement and comfort. He who speaks in a tongue edifies himself, but he who prophesies edifies the church… for you may all prophesy in turn so that everyone may be instructed and encouraged."*

## Quietness/Silence
Habakkuk 2:20 – *But the Lord is in His holy temple; let all the earth be silent before Him."*

Zephaniah 1:7 – *"Be silent before the Sovereign Lord…"*

Psalm 46:10 – *"Be still and know that I am God."*

# Definitions

**Praise** – To commend the worth of; to express approval of

Selected Hebrew words used for praise in the Old Testament:

*Yadah* – to use the hands; to revere or worship with extended hands
*Halal* – to shine, stand out, make a show; to rave or celebrate in ridiculous, absurd praise
*Hallelujah* means *Halal* to Jah, or Jehovah
*Barak* – to kneel; implies blessing God, an act of adoration
*Tehillah* – laudation; praise, especially a hymn of praise
*Zamar* – to touch the strings of an instrument; to praise in song
*Habach* – to address in a loud tone

Selected Greek words used for praise in the New Testament:

*Ainos* – a tale or narration that praises God
*Epainos* – a commendation of the worth of God
*Doxa* – very apparent glory
*Humneo* – to celebrate God in song
*Psallo* – to twitch or twang (as a bowed instrument); sing accompanied songs of praise
*Exomologeo* – a confession of praise; a spoken blessing of God


**Worship** – showing or expressing extreme devotion; having intense love or admiration of any kind

Selected Hebrew words used for worship in the Old Testament:

*Shachah* – to depress (to press down); prostrate on homage to; to fall down flat, to bow down in reverence to
*Cegid* – to prostrate oneself; to worship

Selected Greek words used for worship in the New Testament:
- *Proskuneo* – to do reverence to; to kiss (like a dog licking his master's hand); to humbly adore
- *Sebomai* – to revere, stressing the feeling of awe or devotion; devout, religious worship
- *Doxa* – glory; praise, worship
- *Latreuo* – to minister to God, to serve Him;
- *Enopion* – in the face of; in the presence of

# A Brief Look At Church History And Musical Styles

We sometimes learn invaluable lessons by looking at the past and evaluating the mistakes and successes of our spiritual ancestors. Looking back at the opinions about and reactions to music in the Church is certainly a great place to learn.

Music has been an integral part of the Christian Church from its beginning and, indeed was an integral part of the Hebrew culture in which we are rooted.

Music is one of the most natural and powerful vehicles of expression known to man. It is almost instinctive then that the heart filled with the Holy Spirit and connected to its Maker would express the joy, the yearnings, the wonder, the sorrow, and the outflow of praise to God through music.

There were, of course, differences of opinion in the early Church concerning the nature and use of music in worship. Some leaders became wary of the use of the more expanded forms of worship music. They strove to keep the earlier chant tunes, which were very simple and almost without harmony, as the official music of the Church. They felt that too much attention was being paid to the music to the exclusion of the theology or the expressions of praise in the text.

On the other hand there were leaders who were of the opinion that music could not be allowed to stagnate, making the worship services boring (for that, too, would remove the thoughts of the congregation from the true intent of the worship services!) Therefore, polyphony (harmony) and the use of musical instruments should not be prohibited.

It is difficult for us to imagine today that the use of musical instruments and simple harmony was once considered distracting and even evil, but it is true. The reason it was thought of in this way is largely due to the influence of Greek philosophy in Western thought. The Greek philosophers (Thales, Anaximander, Socrates, Plato, Aristotle) had a tremendous influence on the thought of the early church (and still do). Greek thought was held almost without question in the Church until around 1100 A.D. To understand what the Greeks believed is to understand what many of the early Church fathers believed.

Music meant much more to the ancient Greeks than it does to the 21st century westerner. In the teaching of Pythagoras, Plato and Aristotle, music was a metaphysical entity – a part of the reality of the cosmos, and thus inseparably related to all of the other physical and spiritual aspects of the universe. It wasn't so much an art form as a science, related through mathematical laws to astronomy, geometry and other sciences.

The Greeks thought that music could and did effect the physical universe. They saw that music had the power to sway men's affections and move the hearer to action. From this observation came the need to speak out on the moral qualities of music and its effects on men. They believed that certain modes of music are inherently good while others are inherently bad. If a person habitually listened to "bad" music, he would invariably become a "bad" person. So the musician was held responsible for the effect of his music on the hearer.

Plato went even further and taught that a ban on certain modes of music and certain musical instruments which produce "ignoble passions" was essential. Aristotle was less severe, pointing out that they were not wrong in themselves, but only when used wrongly. These views highly influenced the opinions of the Church fathers in the Middle Ages.

It should be noted that opposition to certain styles of music was not, for the most part, against the use of music, but the abuse of it. They could not argue with the fact that music was constantly written about or used in the Bible, nor that it brought the congregation together in unity and a corporate expression of praise unto God. They were, however, very critical on how music had been used in the secular realm (theatrical performances, etc.) They were cautious and took action to see that the music of the Church did not arouse in the worshiper the same thoughts that pagan music did. John Chrysostum wrote "Thus does the devil stealthily set fire to the city. It is not a matter of running up ladders and using petroleum or pitch or tow: he uses things far more pernicious – lewd sights, base speech, degraded music and songs full of all kinds of wickedness."

So we see that the intention was to separate Church music from worldly music. To do so they thought it best to revert to more primitive forms such as chants and antiphonal singing.

Yet, during the same time period, others such as Basil of Caesarea were praising the effects of music, saying things like: "God mingles the sweetness of harmony with divine truth so that while we are enjoying the pleasures of hearing the music, we may unconsciously gather up the benefits of the words which are being spoken. This is just what a wise doctor will do when, obliged to give bitter medicine to a sick man, he lines the medicine cup with honey." Even St. Ambrose said "Some claim that I have ensnared the people by the melodies of my hymns. I do not deny it." (By the way, heretics also put their doctrine in hymn form I order to spread it abroad.)

St. Augustine conceded that music could be used for good or for evil, but recommended focussing in the positive aspects. He admits, however, that he sometimes struggled with finding the balance; "… whenever it happens that I am more moved by the singing than the thing that is sung, I admit that I have grievously sinned… thus I fluctuate between the peril of indulgence and the profit I have found."

As time passed, musical forms became more complicated. As the use of harmony found it's way into the Church, controversy followed. The Catholic Church finally took a stand in the Papal Edict of 1325, which attacked three areas of modern music: 1) part singing, which was said to "mislead and confuse the simple souls of the congregation", 2) profane music, which combined secular and sacred texts and, 3) certain musical elaborations which were said to distract from the words. The Papacy expressly forbade these musical extravagances in the Church.

The people didn't listen. They seemed to feel that the church was becoming to domineering and putting unnecessary burdens on the people. As the protestant Reformation unfolded, music blossomed, both in secular and sacred arenas. In the early

16th century reformers such as Martin Luther, weary of the oppressions and the heresies of the Catholic Church, broke away from Rome. With this liberation, one change Luther made was the use of more advanced forms of music in the church services. Luther himself was a musician and in his compositions he followed patterns that were often found in secular music. His love for music led him to select forms, albeit "secular" that would cause the people to join in and sing, and to these forms he wrote texts that glorify God. One such song, *A Mighty Fortress Is Our God* is still with us today.

In 1524, Luther wrote "I and several others have brought together certain spiritual songs with a view of spreading abroad and setting in motion the holy Gospel… these, further, are set for four voices for no other reason than that I wished the young might have something to rid them of the opinion that all the arts shall be crushed to the earth and perish through the Gospel, as some bigoted persons pretend, but would willingly see them all, and especially music, servants of Him Who gave and created them."

Luther met opposition from Huldreich Zwingli, who proposed that music should be done away with altogether, and John Calvin, who believed that music should be simple and modest, and to keep it that way, instruments should not be used. The Catholic Church ended up writing their own liturgical music, the way they wanted it, and established these songs as the proper standard for the kind of music to be used in the Church.

**So what does all this mean to us today?**

Some things never change. The debate still goes on today as to what kind of music is the "right" kind to use for worship and evangelistic outreach. There are still those in the Church today who refuse to use musical instruments in their worship. There are those who say that the minor modes are satanic. There are those who oppose "worldly" music in the church. The problem is, who determines what is "worldly" music? Remember, in the Middle Ages it was simple harmony and accompanied singing that was considered "worldly"!

Which kind of music is the right kind to use today? Are there some styles or genres of music that should be banned? What lessons can we learn from history?

Before we begin making assumptions about which musical styles are right or wrong, we should take a moment to contemplate where our assumptions are based. Are they rooted in the metaphysical world of Greek philosophy or in the unchanging truth of the Word of God? The Hebrews viewed music (and, indeed, life) very differently than the Greeks did. They valued essence over form and it was difficult for them to compartmentalize their lives. They did all that they did as worship to God. Music was a natural outflow of their life.

It is very likely that Hebrew music was influenced by and sounded much like, the pagan music of the idolatrous nations that surrounded them. It is also very likely that if those people today who think that music in the minor key is ungodly would have heard the music that David sang to God they would have labeled it an abomination as well. It simply wasn't like our Western music at all. It was weird! (At least to our ears; certainly not to God's!)

I don't think God is all that hung up about styles. I think we are. I also think that our opinions must be recognized as just that… opinions, and that, in the end, we must be anchored to the Word of God to help us discern these issues. So what does the Bible say about all of this?

*The point is not that a certain type of music is inherently wrong, but that it may not be profitable*

I believe that Paul sums it up in 1 Corinthians 6:12 when he says that all things are lawful (allowed) for me, but not all things are profitable. The bottom line is, the language we use must effectively communicate the message we intend to get across. The point is not that a certain type of music is inherently wrong, but that it may not be profitable. Is the music helping or hindering the communication of the message? Is the music so loud that no one can understand the words?

In Romans 14 we are told that there is nothing unclean in itself, but if it causes another person to stumble or fall away from Christ, it is wrong and must be avoided. We cannot lay our burdens (opinions) on others. At the same time, we cannot allow what we call right to be the downfall of another.

Therefore, the language (musical style) we use may depend upon our audience. If I'm ministering to young people in the streets I should use a language they can understand, perhaps a more modern, upbeat music. If I am ministering to folks in a senior citizens home, I had better change the style. All things are allowed, but not all things are profitable.

We have to have the moral maturity as ministers and the musical versatility as musicians to play what will minister most effectively to the hearers and not merely play what we like. Worship is not about what I like…it's about Who I love. And ministry is about loving people enough to get outside ourselves and lead them to God. May God help us to say with Paul "I have become all things to all men so that by all possible means I might save some." (1 Corinthians 9:22b)

# Study Questions

These study questions and points of action are provided as fodder for discussion and practical application of the material presented in the preceding chapters. It has worked well for me in the past to discuss this material in mini teaching sessions at weekly practices or to have teaching Saturdays where we learned and discussed the material.

## What is Worship?
1) In your own words, define worship, particularly as it involves your daily walk with God.
2) In light of the statement, "God is bigger than our present revelation of Him," in what ways do you think your current view of God has limited your worship?
3) When coming to God, is your attitude to give to Him or to receive from Him? To bless Him or to be blessed?

** Point of action: Go down the list of the character qualities of God and do your own study of the nature of God. Let the Holy Spirit increase your understanding of Him as well as your worship vocabulary.

## What Jesus Taught about Worship
1) Why does God emphasize the condition of our heart rather than outward forms of worship?
2) Why is the concept of God being our Father so crucial to our worship?
3) What does it mean to worship both in spirit and in truth? Why is it important to have both in our worship experience?

** Point of action: Spend some time seeking the Lord about worshiping in spirit and in truth. Evaluate lyric content, transparency of the members of your team as well as the degree in which your worship team is "in tune" with the Holy Spirit.

## What Happens When We Worship?
1) What does the word "glory" mean? What does it mean to give God the glory that is due to His name?
2) What are at least six things that God does when we worship Him?
3) How does God use music to edify His Church?
4) What is prophetic worship? How much room do you leave in your worship service for God to speak?

** Point of Action: Use the "Practical tips on Prophetic Worship" appendix to introduce or strengthen the prophetic aspect of your worship service.

## Levitical Worship
1) What is meant by the statement "Musicians are plentiful but worshipers are few?"
2) What does it mean to be a "bearer of the presence"?
3) Explain in your own words what it means to be consecrated.

** Point of action: Outline the steps in the consecration ceremony of the Levites and how it applies to us today.

## Seven Spirits of a Worshiper
1) Would those closest to me say that I am characterized by humility?
2) Evaluate your relationships with fellow worship team members. Are you one under authority? If you are in a position of authority, are you responsible to walk in that authority as a servant to those who are "under your hands?"
3) What are the differences between anointing, ability, and authority?
4) Is your integrity such that people can receive from your ministry?

** Point of Action: As a group discuss the following: What can each one of you do *this week* to begin increasing your skill on your instrument? (remember that if you are a vocalist, your voice is your instrument)
*What can you do this month? Over the next five years?*

## Priming Your Praise Pump
1) Honestly, do you prepare an offering to bring to the Lord, or do you just show up?
2) In reading this section, what way do you see that Satan attempts to steal your worship?
3) What can you pro-actively do to stop him from stealing your worship?

** Point of Action: Purpose as a group to dedicate the next six weeks to being faithful to prepare an offering to bring to the Lord in your corporate worship meetings.

## Worship in the Life of David
1) In what ways does self-control effect our worship?
2) Is God revealing areas where you need His grace in controlling your thought life?
3) Do you see any parallels between David's life and yours? (praising Him in all seasons, repentance, passion for God's presence, etc.)
4) What is a secret life with God?

## Why We Worship the Way We Do
** Point of Action: Spend time as a team going over all of these Biblical expressions of worship. It is important that we know why we do what we do. How can these truths be communicated to your congregation? (We have tried teaching them in small home groups, printing up cards to hand out to visitors and make available to the congregation that have these scriptures on them... be creative!)

# Section Two

# Music Theory Applied to Worship

# Understanding Music Theory

As a worship leader or praise team member, a fundamental understanding of music theory can be your best friend. Normally there are two categories that someone reading this book might fall into:

1) "Legit (legitimate) players," or those who have learned to play by way of formal music lessons, usually involving the learning of fundamentals by a teacher and/or a book in a step-by-step approach.

2) "Ear players," or those who have had little or no formal training, but have the ability to pick up the essentials on their own by trial and error, listening and duplicating what they hear.

Both categories have strengths and weaknesses. Legit players have the advantage of being able, at least to some degree, to read music. This gives them a head start in understanding the elements of pitch, rhythm and dynamics and how they are notated on a score. The main disadvantage for legit players that cannot play by ear is that they are basically bound to their written music. If it is not written down in front of them, they cannot play it. Many times they freeze up when asked to play even a simple piece if there is no music to read. Also, generally speaking, those who do not play by ear tend to play stiffly and mechanically.

Ear players have the advantage of being able to hear a piece and find the chord progression and melody easily. By and large they not only can reproduce the musical sounds, but also the musical *feel* of the song. Of course, the inherent weakness is that they cannot sight read a piece of music and, because they lack the musical vocabulary, they usually are limited in their ability to communicate what they hear, or want to hear from other players or singers. It seems that they can go only so far, but no further. They are often frustrated because of this.

The good news is that there is an answer! This section attempts to solve the problems and strengthen the weaknesses inherent in both legit and ear players by teaching simple music theory. I have taught musicians from both extremes for many years and I love to see the eyes light up when they see how a little music theory opens their world up and creates a new ability to express themselves to the Lord.

In this section we are going to learn three basic elements of music theory:

| Pitch | What notes or notes you play (high or low) | WHAT YOU PLAY |
|---|---|---|
| Rhythm | Duration of time in which you play pitches | WHEN YOU PLAY |
| Dynamics | The volume or "feel" with which you play | HOW YOU PLAY IT |

# Rhythm

PITCH has to do with what note you play. RHYTHM has to do with when and how long you play it. Music is divided into equal parts called measures. BAR LINES indicate the beginning and end of a measure. Double bar lines separate sections and double bar lines, one thick and one thin, show the end of a piece.

TIME SIGNATURES are placed at the beginning of a piece of music. They contain two numbers. The top number shows the number of beats (or counts) in each measure. The bottom number what kind of a note gets one beat.

For example: $\frac{4}{4}$ means there are 4 quarter notes in each measure (also notated C for "common time")

$\frac{3}{4}$ means there are 3 quarter notes in each measure

$\frac{6}{8}$ means there are 6 eighth notes in each measure

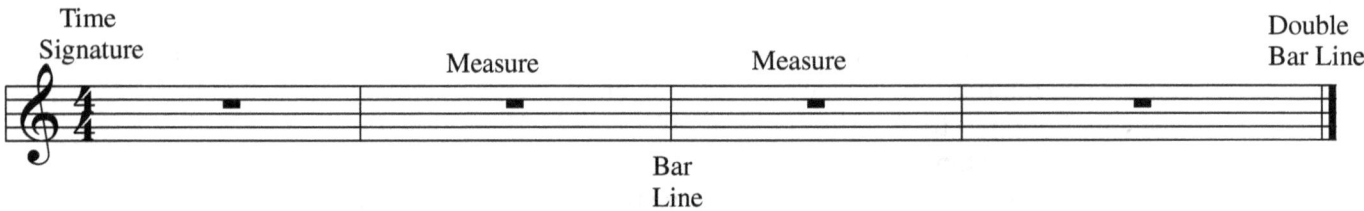

**The duration of musical sounds (long and short) is indicated by different types of notes.**

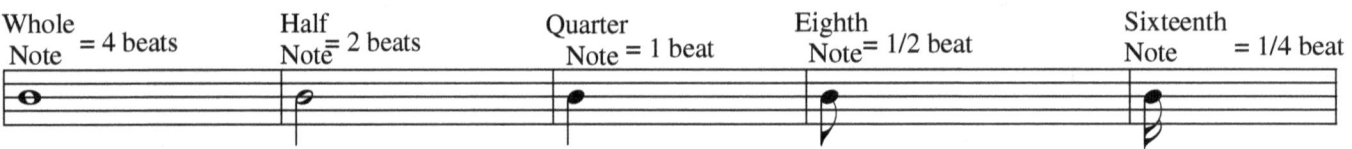

So, in order to fill up a $\frac{4}{4}$ measure you add any combination of notes whose sum equals 4 beats.

# Dotted Notes

A DOT placed after any note adds one half the value of the original note. For example, a quarter note gets one beat. A dotted quarter note gets one and one half beats. Similarly, a half note gets two beats while a dotted half note gets is held out for three beats.

# Tied Notes

The same effect can be accomplished using a TIE. A tie is a curved line that connects two adjacent notes of the same pitch. The tone is held as though the two notes are one. The tied rhythms below are the same as the dotted ones above.

# Rests

A REST is a period of silence in music. The duration of rests coincide with the duration of musical notes, therefore, there are whole, half, quarter, eighth and sixteenth rests. To fill a $\frac{4}{4}$ measure you add any combination of rests whose sum equals four beats.

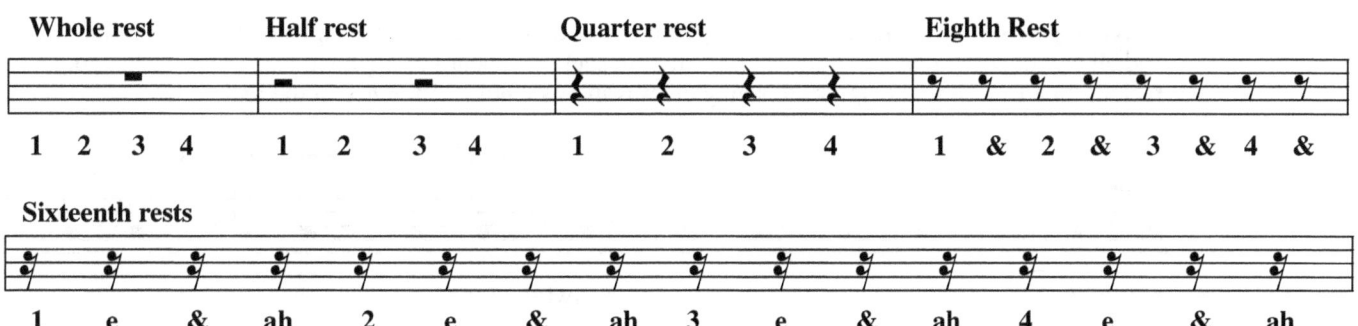

# Syncopation

At times the accents in a song will fall on normally weak divisions of the beat. This is called SYNCOPATION and it adds punch and excitement to your music. Below are some examples of syncopated beats.

# Triplets

A triplet is a group of three notes that are played in the space normally allotted for two of the same kind of note. For example, two eighth notes are two notes in the space of one beat whereas three eighth note triplets are three notes in the space of one beat. Similarly, quarter note triplets are three notes in the space of one half note.

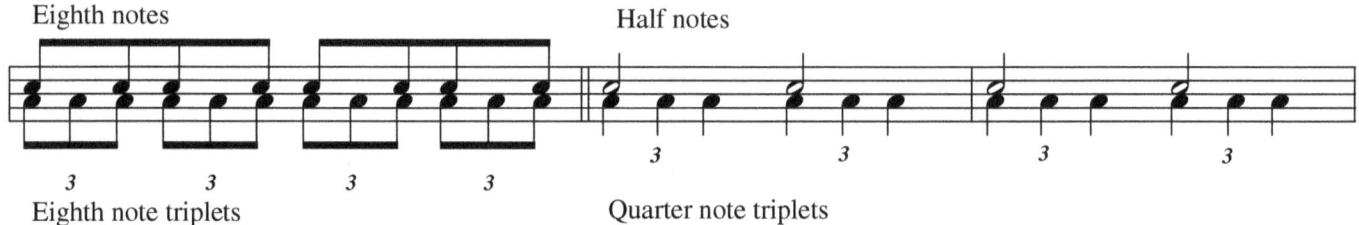

# Swing Eighths

When you play swing time you play eighth notes as though they were a triplet consisting of a quarter note and an eighth note. This creates a "swing" rhythm such as is heard in big band jazz music. Changing a simple melody line from straight eighths to swing eighths makes a huge difference in the feel of the song.

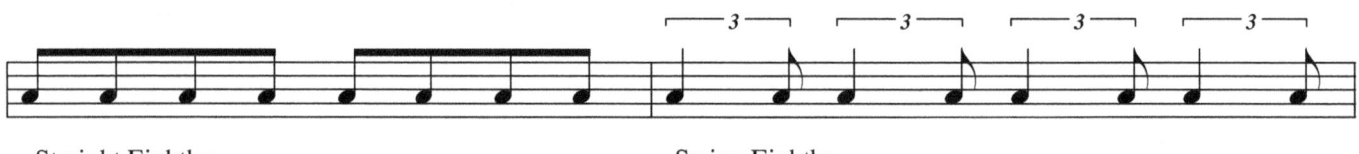

# Pitch

## Music Notation

In order to communicate in the written language of music it is necessary to learn the standard form of music notation. Music is written on a five line STAFF. Between each line there is a space. There are four spaces on a staff. Musical sounds are shown by the position of the notes on the staff. The higher the note, the higher the sound. The lower the note, the lower the sound.

At the beginning of each staff is a CLEF. The treble staff contains the higher sounds or pitches while the bass staff contains the lower ones. When the two staffs are joined together they form the GRAND STAFF.

A LEGER LINE is a small line which is added above or below either the treble or bass staffs. The note middle C is on the first leger line below the treble staff. Middle C is also notated on the first leger line above the bass staff.

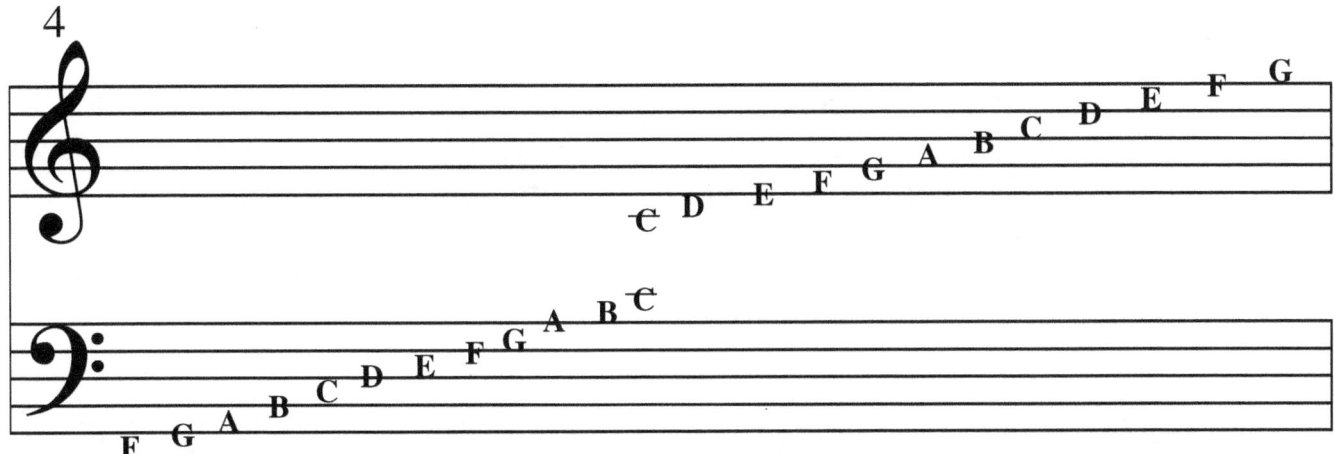

Grand Staff

# Notes of the Grand Staff

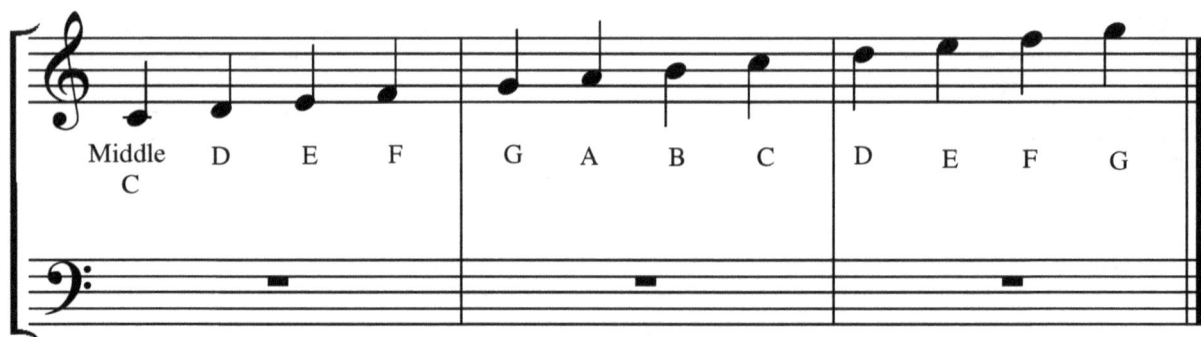

## Accidentals

A FLAT SIGN (b) lowers the pitch of the note it is in front of by a half step (one tone lower). A SHARP SIGN (#) raises the pitch of the note it is in front of by a half step (one tone higher). A NATURAL SIGN (♮) cancels the effect of a flat or a sharp. Flats, sharps and naturals are centered on the line or space which they effect. When placed before a note, they affect every note on the same line or space for an entire measure. The bar line cancels the effect of an accidental. (See Fig. 6)

**Fig. 6**

# Intervals

An INTERVAL is the distance between two notes. A HALF STEP is the distance from a note to the closest note above or below it (C to Db, F to E, etc.). A WHOLE STEP is equal to two half steps (C to D, F to Eb, etc.). Most scales are built out of whole steps and half steps.

All intervals can be measured in half steps. On a keyboard, begin counting the first note as zero, then count half steps until you reach the correct number for the interval you are looking for. Here are a few examples: The major third above a C is an E; The minor sixth from an F is a Db; The major second from an E is an F#. (See Fig. 4)

**Fig.4**

| # Of Half Steps | Interval Name |
|---|---|
| 0 | Perfect Unison |
| 1 | Minor Second |
| 2 | Major Second |
| 3 | Minor Third |
| 4 | Major Third |
| 5 | Perfect Fourth |
| 6 | Augmented Fourth or Diminished Fifth |
| 7 | Perfect Fifth |
| 8 | Minor Sixth |
| 9 | Major Sixth |
| 10 | Minor Seventh |
| 11 | Major Seventh |
| 12 | Perfect Octave |

You can also measure an interval by looking at the musical staff. Designating the first note as "one", count up the lines and spaces until you reach the second note in the interval. If this note is within the major scale (we will cover major scales next) then it is a MAJOR interval. If it is a lowered note, it is a MINOR or DIMINISHED interval. If it is a raised note, it is an AUGMENTED interval. (See Fig. 5)

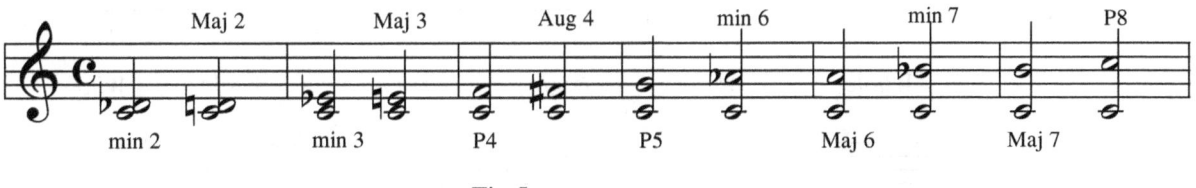

Fig.5

# Major Scale Construction

The MAJOR SCALE is made up of eight consecutive tones in alphabetical order, from "do" to "do" one octave higher.

```
                                              B (ti)   C (do)
                                     A (la)
                            G (so)
                    F (fa)
            E (me)
     D (re)
C (do)
```

If you start at C and go up the keyboard playing the white notes until you reach the next C, you have played a major scale. Notice that the Major Scale is made up of a pattern of half steps (Notes next to each other) and whole steps (notes with a note between them) starting from C, the pattern is *Whole, Whole, Half, Whole, Whole, Whole, Half.*

```
   Whole    Whole              Whole    Whole    Whole
 C        D        E        F        G        A        B        C
                    Half                                    Half
```

The pattern we see in the key of C is the same for any major scale, no matter which note you start on. Pick any note and count up using this pattern and you will hear a Major Scale. Note that you will have to add accidentals (sharps or flats) in order to keep the pattern true. Below you can see the Major Sale pattern used to construct Major Scales in the keys of C, G and Ab.

# Major Scales (Flat Keys)

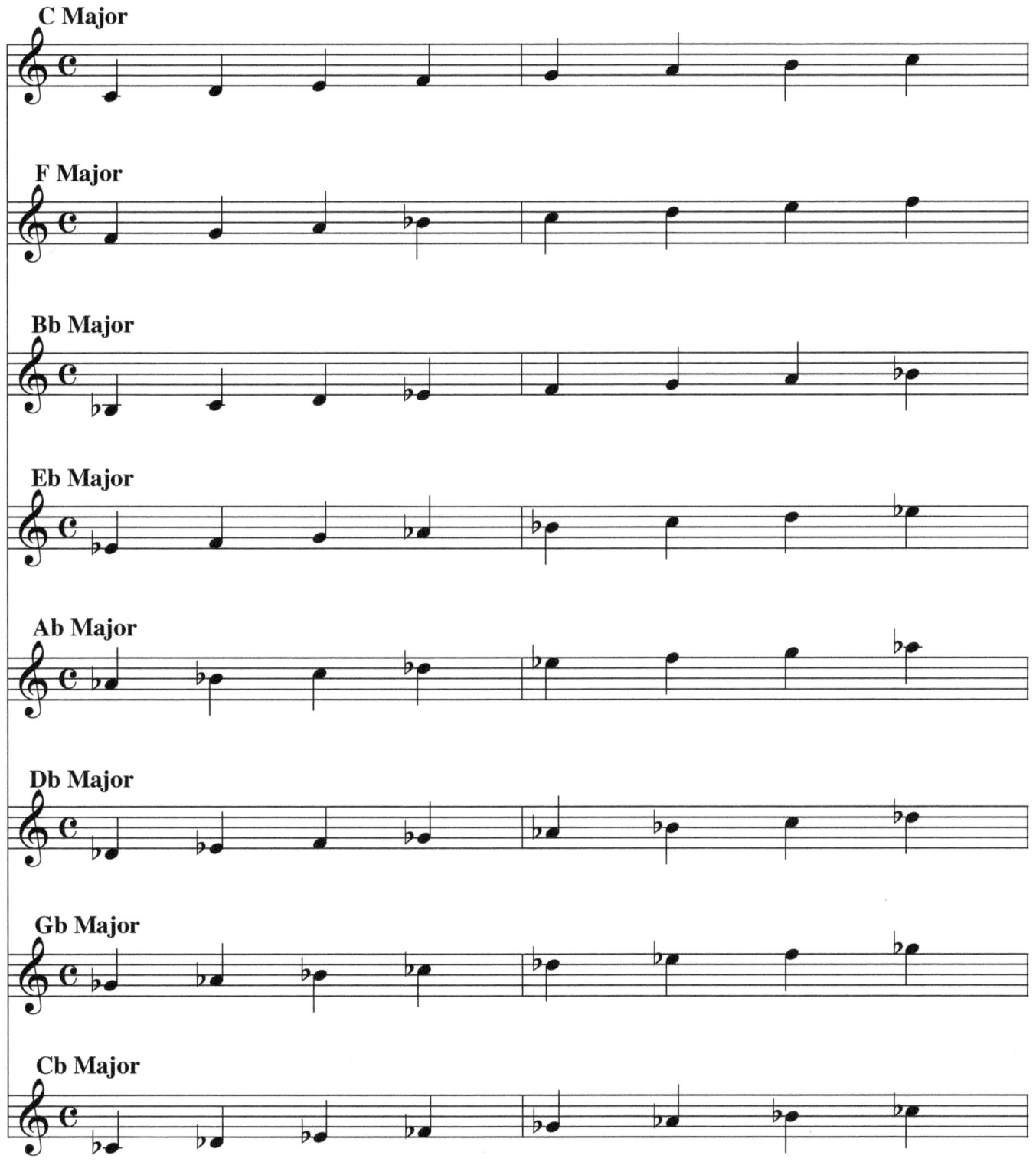

# Major Scales (Sharp Keys)

# Key Signatures

When we constructed Major Scales, we wrote the sharps and flats before each note in on the staff. In order to make the writing process easier, we can indicate the flats and sharps to be used in a composition at the beginning of the piece. This is called a KEY SIGNATURE. The key signature tells the performer that the accidentals indicated are in effect throughout the entire piece.

For example, the key of G has one sharp in it (F#). The sharp that appears on the top line of the staff indicates that all of the F's in this piece are to be sharped.

Below are the key signatures for every major key.

## Sharp Key Signatures

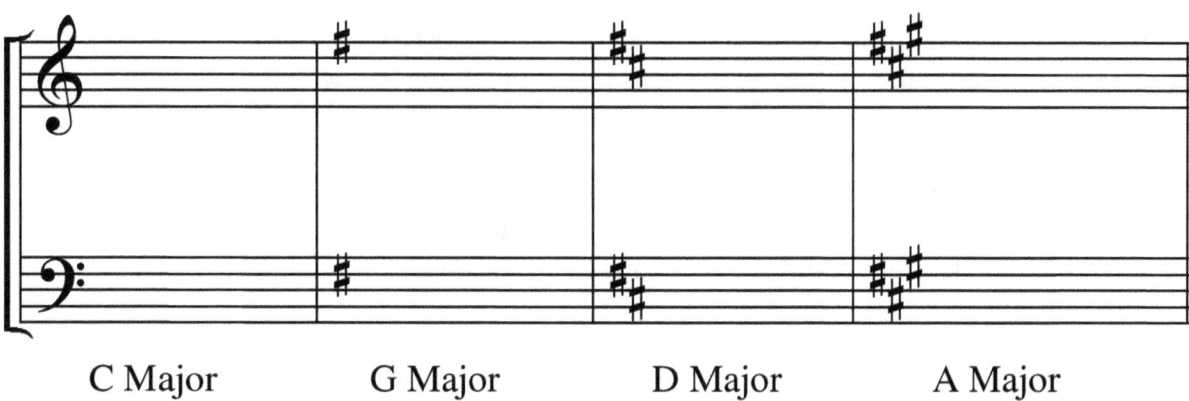

C Major      G Major      D Major      A Major

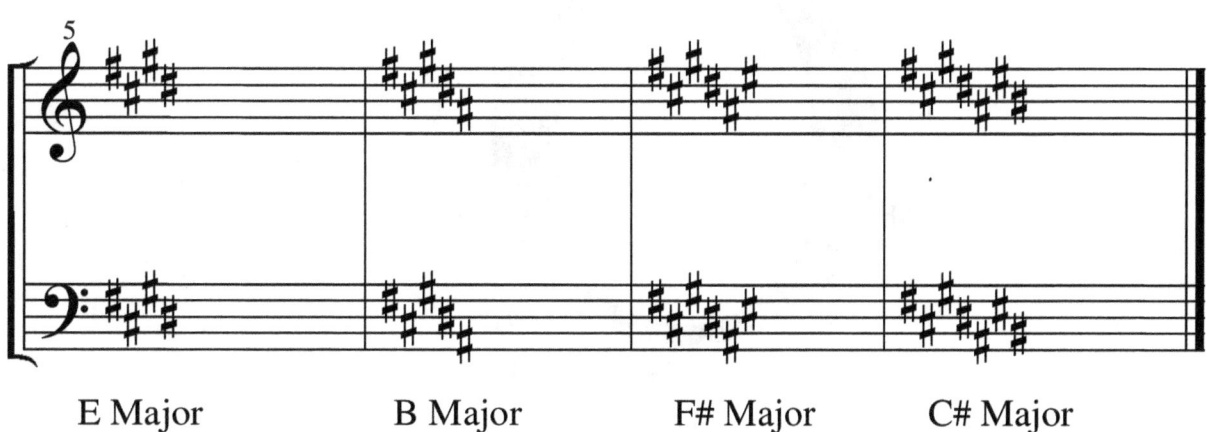

E Major      B Major      F# Major      C# Major

# Flat Key Signatures

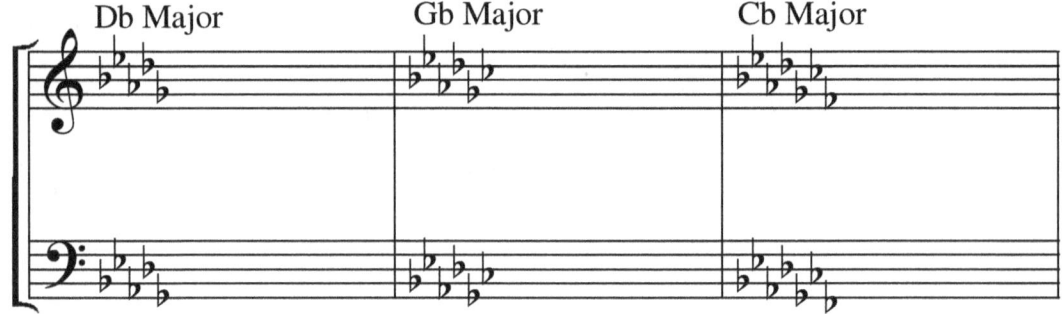

**Circle of Fifths**

Keys are related by fifths. If we start on C (no sharps or flats) and go up the scale five notes we come to G (1 sharp). Go up five more notes and we come to D (2 sharps). This pattern continues throughout the sharp keys. Conversely, if we start on C and go down five notes we come to F (1 flat), etc. When we put all the sharp and flat keys together we have the CIRCLE OF FIFTHS. The most common interval of chord movement is the fifth. Memorizing the Circle of Fifths will help you in understanding and hearing chord progressions as well as remembering how many sharps and flats are in a given key.

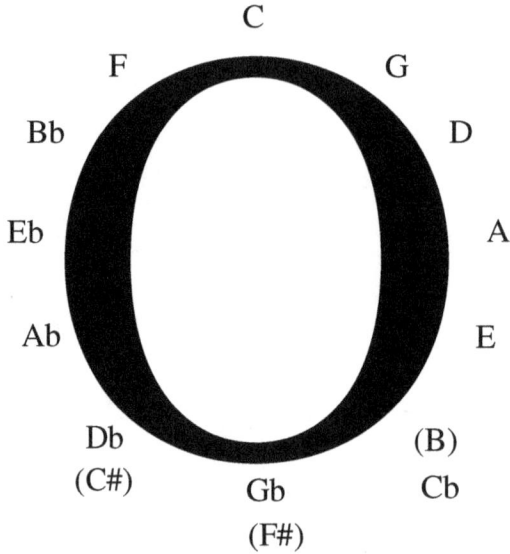

# Triads and Seventh Chords

A CHORD is a combination of three or more tones sounded simultaneously. A TRIAD is a 3-note chord. A MAJOR TRIAD is constructed of the 1st, 3rd, and 5th tones of a major scale.

Other triads are derived by altering the major chord. For example, to make a MINOR TRIAD, we take a major triad and lower the 3rd by one half step; to make a DIMINISHED TRIAD, take a major triad and lower the 3rd and the 5th by one half step each; to make an AUGMENTED TRIAD, raise the 5th of a major triad by one half step; a suspended, or SUS CHORD is made by replacing the 3rd of a major triad with a 4th, and a 9 (or a 2) chord is made by replacing the 3rd of a major triad with a 2nd. These are the most common triads you will encounter.

Since the pattern for constructing a major scale is the same in every key, the method of constructing triads is also the same. Where you start doesn't matter. Just hold true to the pattern and you will build the chords correctly. Below are major, minor, diminished, augmented, sus and 9 chords in three different keys. Construct and practice these chords in all keys.

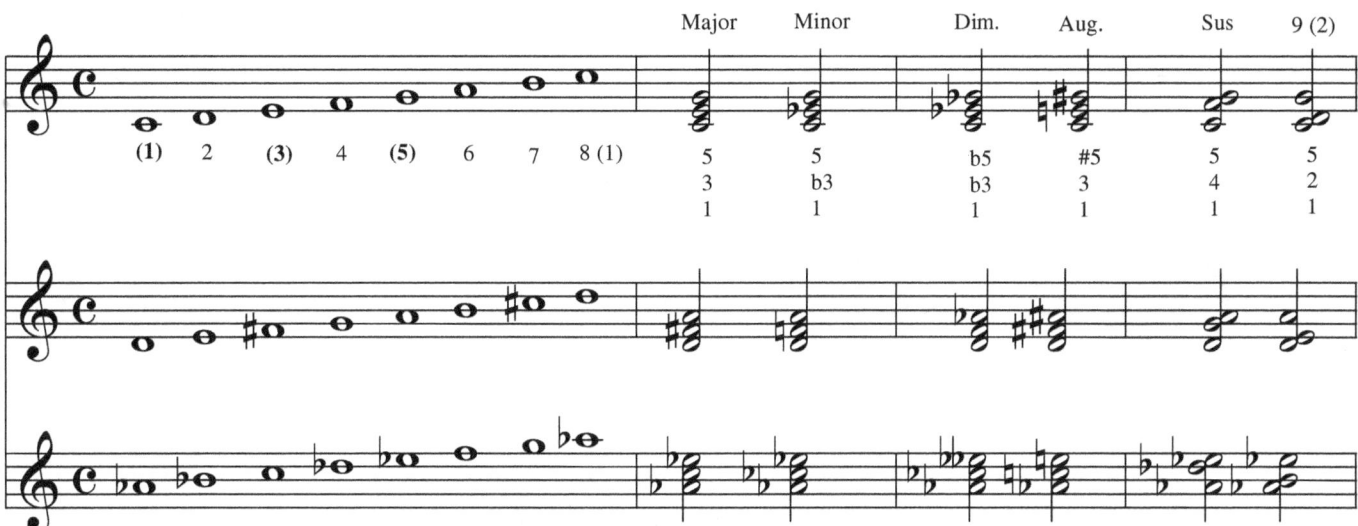

Similarly, we can construct a MAJOR 7th chord by using the 1st, 3rd, 5th and 7th notes of the major scale. A DOMINANT 7th chord is derived by lowering the 7th tone by one half step (1,3,5,b7). A MINOR 7th is 1,b3,5,b7. A MINOR 7th(b5) is 1,b3,b5,b7. A DIMINISHED 7th is 1,b3,b5,bb7. These are the most common seventh chords you will see. Below are Seventh Chords in the keys of C, D and Ab. Practice these chords also in all keys.

# Inversions

The way the notes of a chord are arranged is known as the chord's VOICING. It is both impractical and poor sounding to play all triads and seventh chords in root position (stacked in third intervals, 1,3,5 or 1,3,5,7). To make the chord progressions easier to play and to make them sound better, we can rearrange the order of the notes. Rearranged chords are called INVERSIONS.

If we take the bottom note and place it on top (so that the third is on the bottom) it is called 1st inversion. If we take the bottom note of that chord and put it on top (so that the 5th is on the bottom) it is in 2nd inversion. If we have a seventh chord, we can invert in once more (so that the 7th in on the bottom) and we have 3rd inversion.

Most of the time, when you see "slash" chords written into a piece of music they are indicating that an inversion of a chord is to be played  For example: C/E means to play a C major chord with an E as the bass, or lowest note in the voicing. Similarly, a Gmin/Bb indicates that a G minor chord with a Bb in the bass is to be played.

**Triad Inversions**

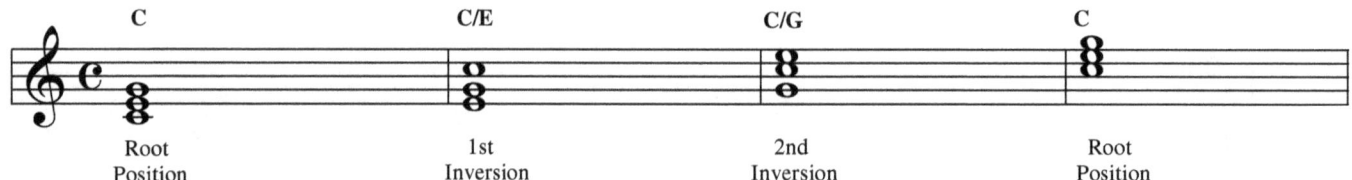

**Seventh Chord Inversions**

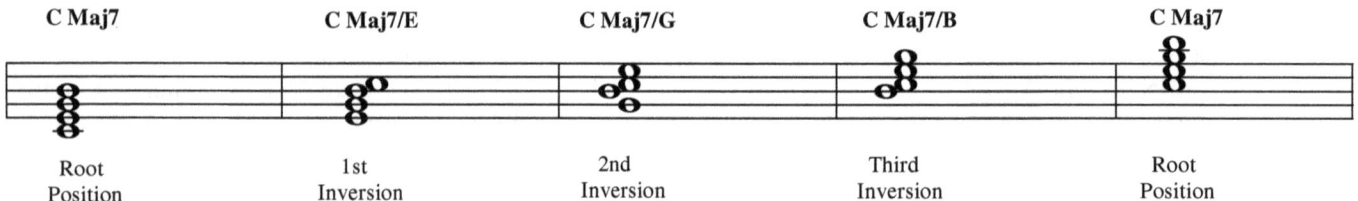

By using inversions, that is, different chord VOICINGS, we can make a chord progression flow smoother and sound better. This is called VOICE LEADING. Notice that the two progressions below are the same. However, the second one will sound much smoother because of the use of inversions to create good VOICE LEADING.

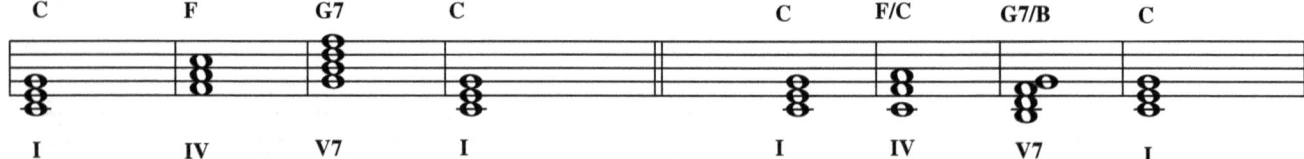

# Diatonic Harmony
(Chords Within A Key)

If we take a major scale and stack notes up in third intervals on each note of the scale (making a triad on each note), and staying true to the key signature, we see a series of chords which are within the key, or DIATONIC. These are the most common chords that will be used in a song which is in that key. Note that since we are staying true to the key signature, different chord qualities are in the series (some are major, some minor and one is diminished).

To help us see how the chords relate within the key, we identify them by using Roman numerals (Upper case for major chords and lower case for minor chords). Since the pattern for constructing the major scale is the same in all keys, the pattern of the diatonic chords is the same in all keys. The pattern is:

$$\begin{aligned}
\text{I} &= \text{Major} \\
\text{ii} &= \text{minor} \\
\text{iii} &= \text{minor} \\
\text{IV} &= \text{Major} \\
\text{V} &= \text{Major} \\
\text{vi} &= \text{minor} \\
\text{vii} &= \text{diminished}
\end{aligned}$$

Below are the diatonic triads for each of the flat keys. These are the most commmon chords (but not the only chords) that you will encounter in each of these keys. Memorizing these and playing them on your instrument will greatly help you to understand chord progressions and memorizing songs.

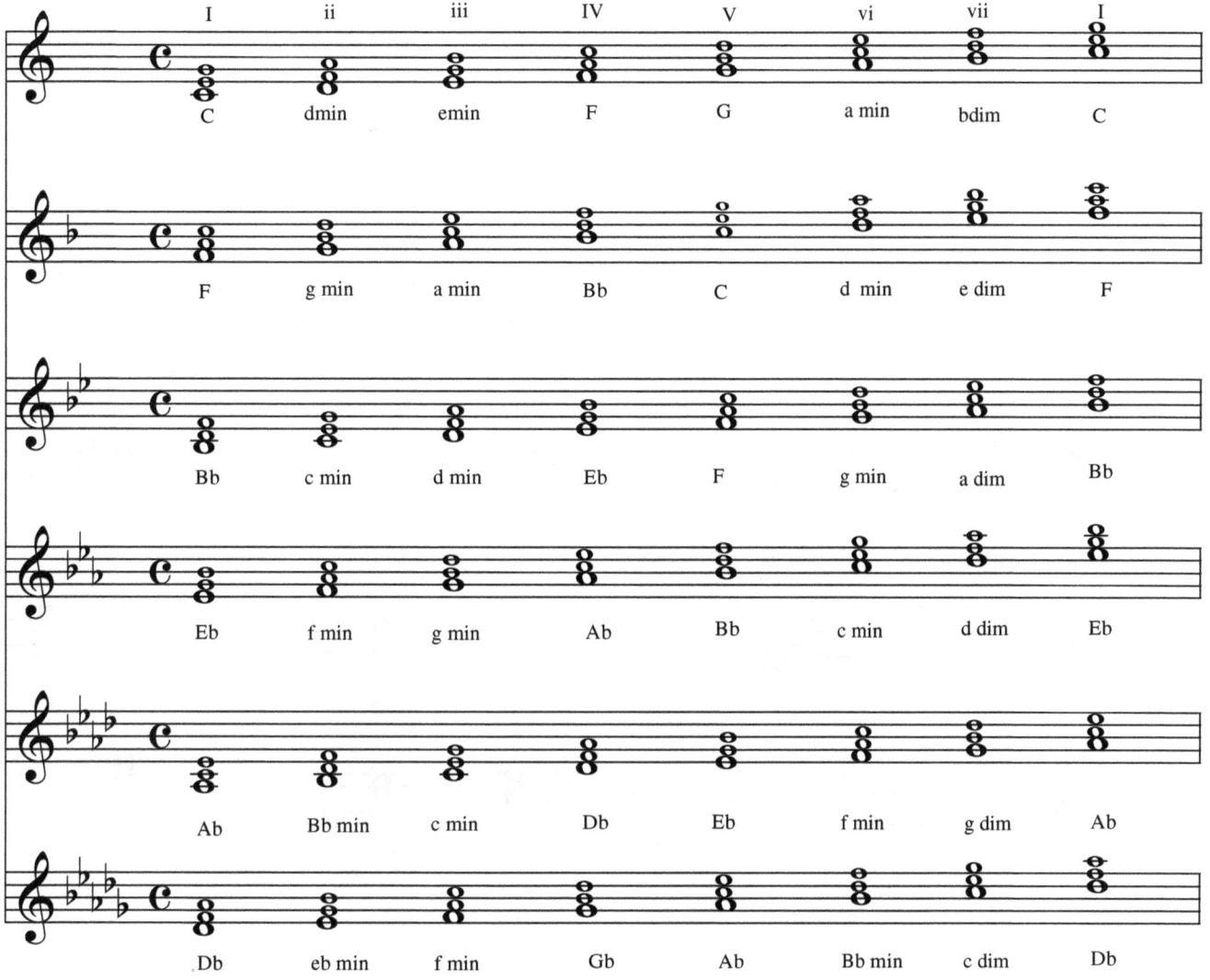

# Diatonic Triads (Sharp Keys)

Below are the diatonic triads (most common chords) for the sharp keys. These, together with the preceeding page, represent all of the most common chords in all keys.

Note that three keys, Gb, Cb and C# are not included. This is because these keys are represented by the keys of F#, B and Db, respectively. When two notes (or chords) that sound the same, are spelled differently, they are called ENHARMONICS (e.g. F#, Gb). This is why you may hear it said that there are 12 keys or that there are 15 keys. Technically, there are 15 keys, but practically speaking, there are only 12.

Writing these enharmonic keys out would be redundant, since learning the fingerings in one key will result in you knowing them in its enharmonic equivalent. However, it is important that you learn these chords from both reference points (thinking in the key of Gb and in the key of F#). Refer to the Transposition Chart to see the diatonic progressions in all 15 keys.

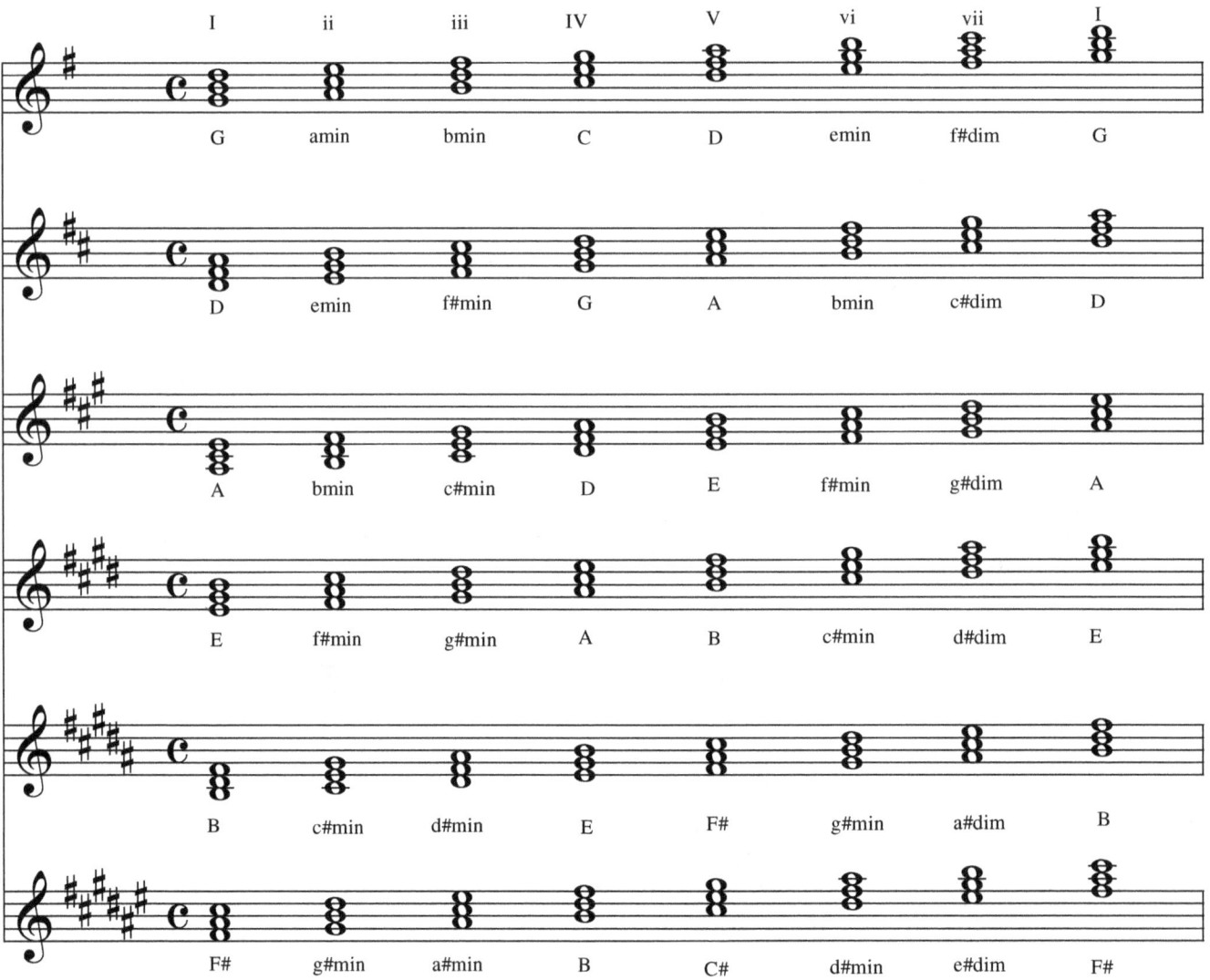

# Diatonic Seventh Chords

Just as we created diatonic triads by building triads on each degree of the major scale, we can also create diatonic 7th chords by building 7th chords on each degree of the major scale. The pattern for diatonic 7th chords is also the same in all keys:

**I = Major 7th**
**ii = minor 7th**
**iii = min 7th**
**IV = Major 7th**
**V = Dominant 7th**
**vi = minor 7th**
**vii = minor 7th (b5)**

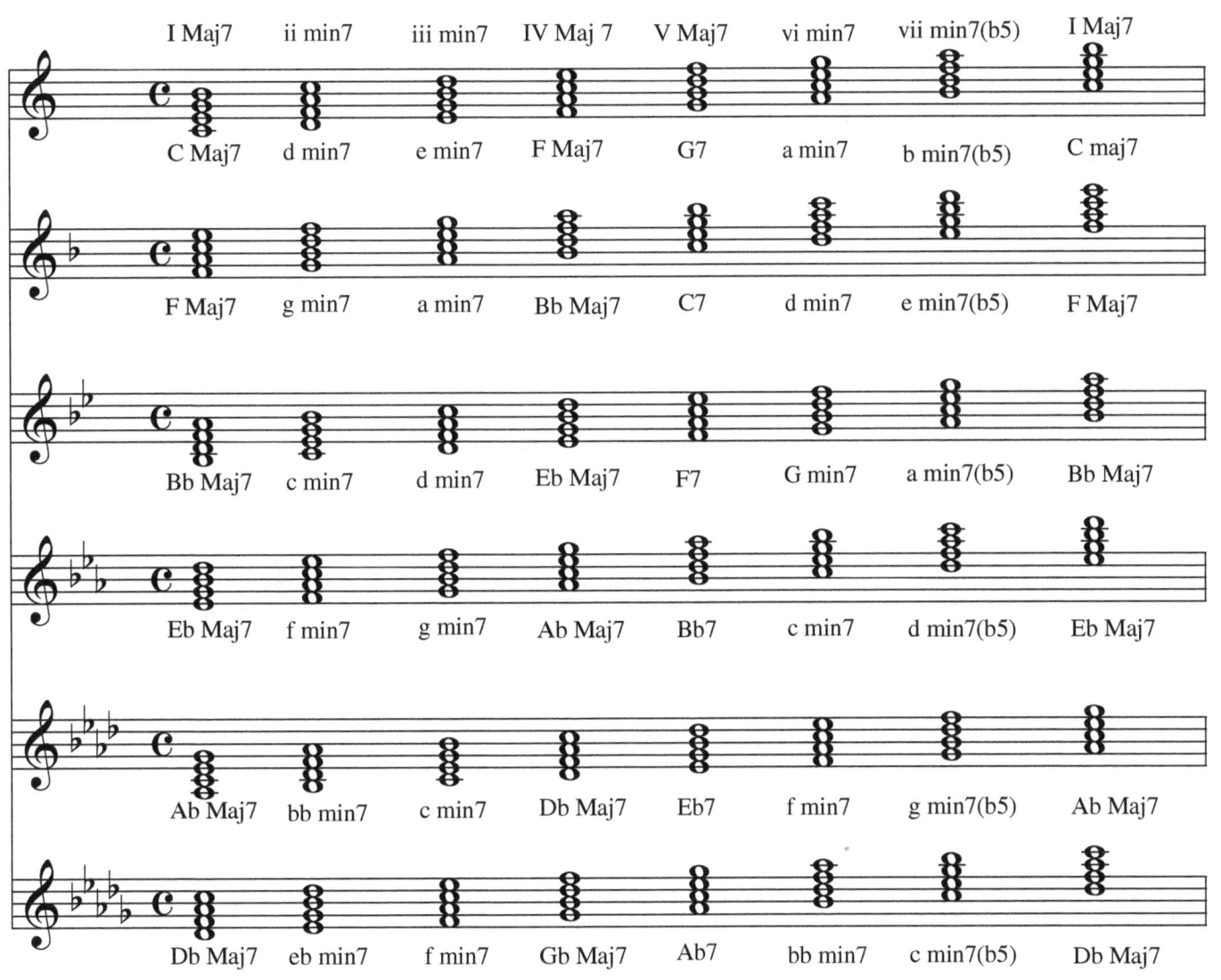

# Diatonic Seventh Chords
## (Sharp Keys)

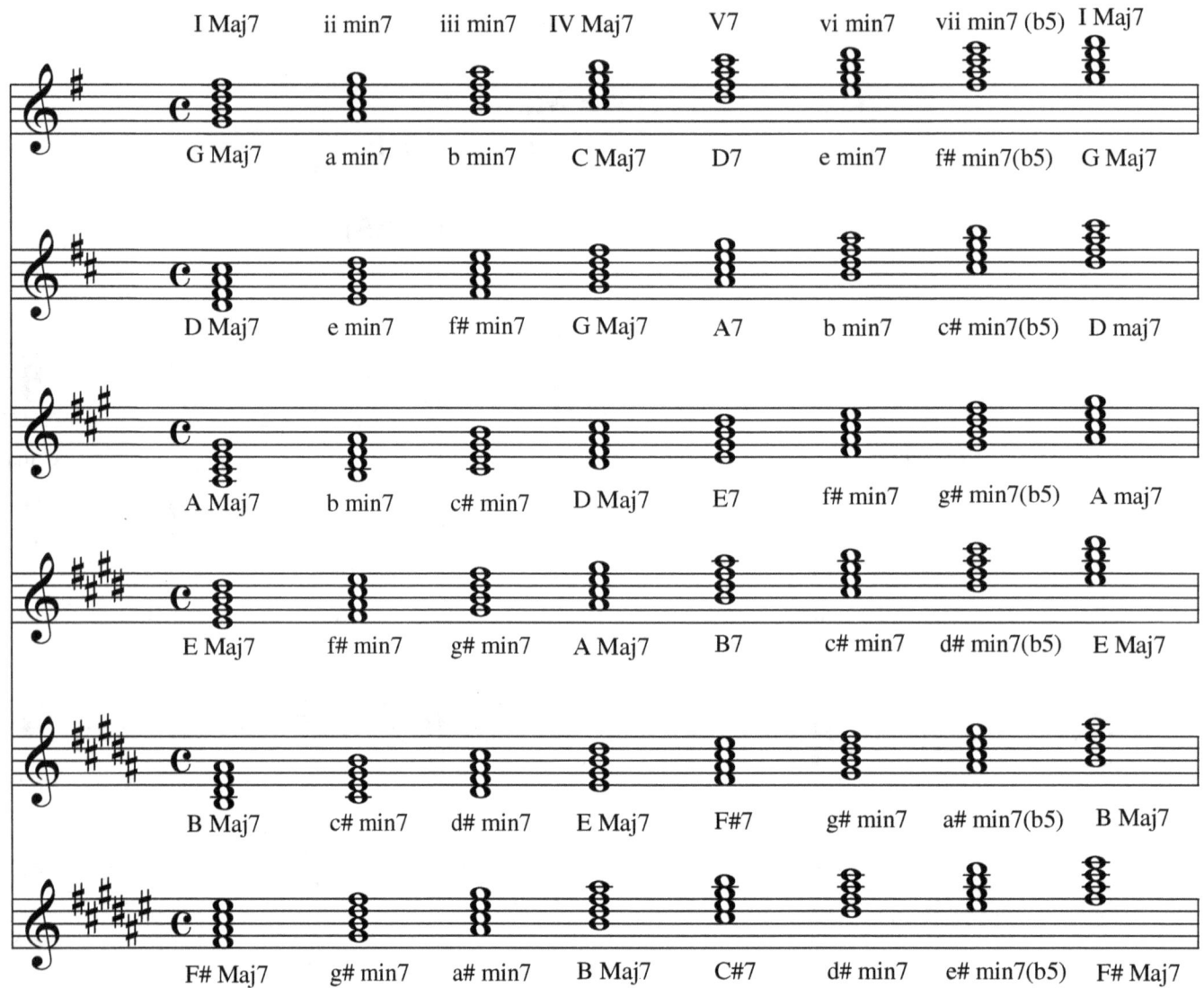

# Voicing Diatonic Triads and Seventh Chords)

Now that we know which triads and seventh chords are in each key, we need to know how to voice them so that they sound well. When playing triads, the 1,1,3,5 voicing produces a smooth sound. In this voicing the left hand plays the root of the chord twice (using the fifth finger [pinky] and the thumb), while the right hand plays the 3rd and the 5th (using the thumb and third [middle finger])

When playing seventh chords, the 1,7,3,5 voicing sounds well. In this voicing, the root and the 7th are played by the left hand (using the fifth finger and the thumb) and the 3rd and 5th are played with the right hand (thumb and third finger)

Below is an example of diatonic triads and seventh chords using this fingering. Color tones can also be added by using your remaining fingers. Practice these voicings in all keys and you will have a foundational way to finger nearly any chord progression.

## C Major diatonic triads (1,1,3,5 voicing)

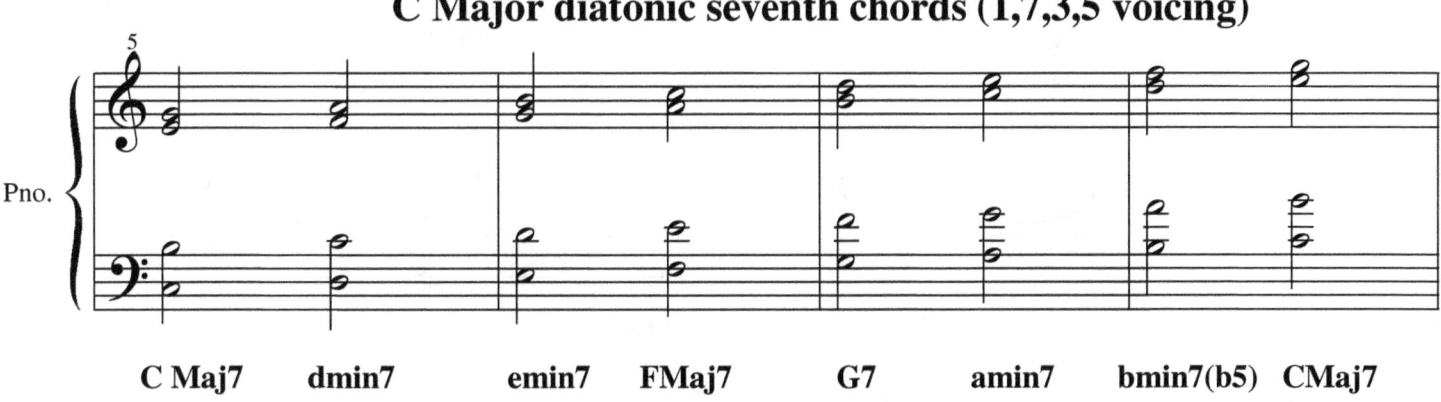

## C Major diatonic seventh chords (1,7,3,5 voicing)

# How to Learn a Song Quickly

It is relatively easy to learn a song quickly when you understand diatonic harmony. The simplest way to think of it is that there are only two places in music: "Home" and "away from home." Home is the key note of the key you are in, or the "I chord". For example, "C" in the key of C; "Eb" in the key of Eb, etc. Away is anywhere else.

Generally speaking (but not always), a song starts at home and ends up at home. In between, there are 4 or 8 measure phrases which wander away from home and back to home.

## Recognizing the Song Form

When learning a piece of music, think in phrases, instead of individual notes or chords. Just as we talk or read in phrases, sentences and paragraphs, we read and play music in much the same way.

Perhaps the best way to explain it is this: if you were trying to map the outline of an island in the ocean, it would be extremely difficult to do so while walking around the perimeter of the shoreline. You just can't get the right perspective from there. It would be much easier if you were in a helicopter hovering above the island. From there you can clearly see the outline and reproduce it. It's the same with a song. If you back up, look a at the overview, or the big picture, you can get perspective on the form.

So, when approaching a song, we want to back up, think in phrases and look for repetition. Worship songs usually have forms made up of sections, such as verses, choruses and bridges. Think of the first section as the "A" section and any distinctly different sounding section as a "B" section. Some songs even have third sections ("C" sections).

## Thinking Within the Key (Thinking Diatonically)

If you know what key you are in, you automatically narrow down the chord possibilities. For example, the key of C Major will probably not contain an Eb chord, simply because there are no sharps or flats in the key of C Major. This is not to say that you will never encounter chords that are outside the key, but that the most common chords will be diatonic, or within the key. It helps to think in numbers (I, IV, V vi, etc.). Notice how we use numbers in the chord progression of "Amazing Grace", below.

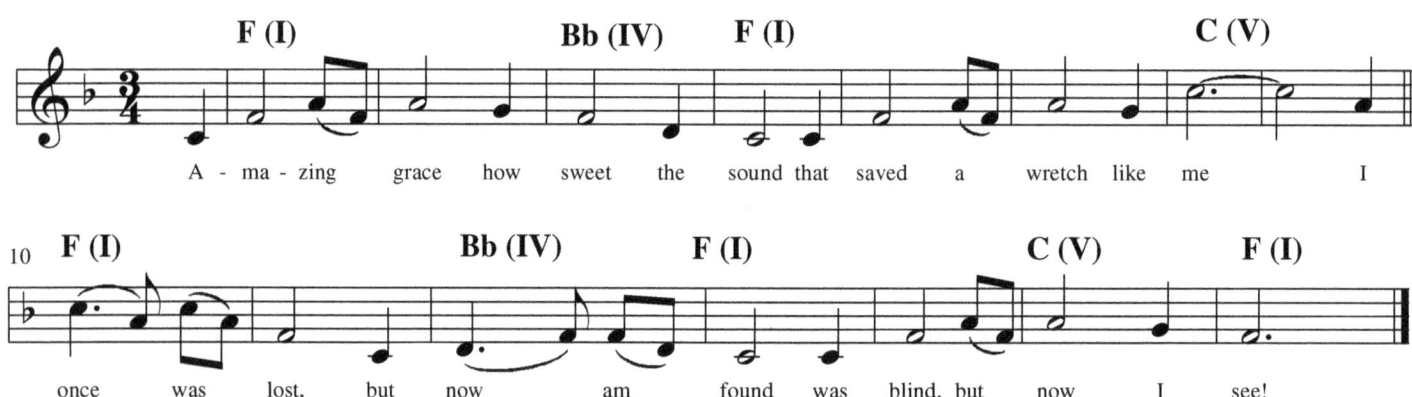

102

# Functional Harmony

The seven diatonic chords in each major key can be divided into three categories of harmonic function: Tonic, Dominint and Sub-Dominant. Generally speaking, we associate the I chord and the vi chord as the TONIC, the V chord and the vii chord as the DOMINANT and the ii or the IV chord as the SUBDOMINANT.

Remember that we stated that there are only two places in musuc: home and away from home, and that a song will usually start out at home (the key note) and move away from there and back to there several times during the progression. In Western music (as opposed to Eastern or "Oriental" music) our chord progressions tend to move from subdominant to dominant to tonic. That is why we see so many IV, V, I or ii, V, I progressions in our songs. Our ears have been trained to hear harmony flow in that sequence. Understanding this tendency for the chord progression to flow from subdominant to dominant to tonic will help you in memorizing chord progressions and in learning to pick out songs by ear.

If you play the progression iii, vi, ii, V, I in any key you will see what I mean. As you play the chords, your ear can almost hear what the next chord should be even before you play it. This is not to say that chords always flow in this direction (there is never an "always" in music.) Sometimes the V will go to a vi chord; sometimes the IV will go to the I chord; I chords can go anywhere they want to go, and so on, but generally, this is the way harmony flows.

$$iii \longrightarrow vi \longrightarrow \begin{bmatrix} ii \\ IV \end{bmatrix} \longrightarrow \begin{bmatrix} V \\ vii \end{bmatrix} \longrightarrow I$$

(Subdominant)    (Dominant)    (Tonic)

# Form in Music

Most songs can be broken down into sections. It is helpful to recognize and mentally separate the verses, choruses, bridges, "pre-choruses", musical interludes and any other sections of a song. For reference sake, you may label the verse of a song the "A section" and the chorus a "B section". Sometimes songs will have a specific form such as AABA (a four bar phrase (A section) that repeats followed by a completely different phrase (B section) followed by another A section). The worship song "As the Deer" by Marty Nystrom is a good example of an AABA song. Other forms you might see are ABA, ABAB, or ABCA. Some songs have no recognizable form. These are called THROUGH COMPOSED.

There are other symbols that indicate the form of a song.

    D.C. (Da Capo) means go back to the beginning

    D.S. (Dal Signo) means go back to the sign ( 𝄋 )

    Fine (fee-nay) means the end

If we put them together:

    D.C. al fine means Go back to the beginning, play to the fine sign

    D.S. al fine means go back to the (𝄋) and play to the fine sign

Sometimes a song will end with a separate closing section, called a Coda and indicated by the ⊕ sign.

REPEAT SIGNS and 1ST and 2ND ENDINGS are also used to indicate the form of a song. In the example below, the passage is played to the repeat sign, then started over. The second time through, the second ending is taken instead of the 1st ending, and the song is finished.

(Repeat Sign)

# Transposing

So we can see that there are only three chords in the song "Amazing Grace", the I chord, the IV chord, and the V chord. Since the chords in a key are relative to the starting pitch and the major scale pattern is the same in any key, we can use the Roman numerals to find the corect chords in another key. This is called TRANSPOSING.

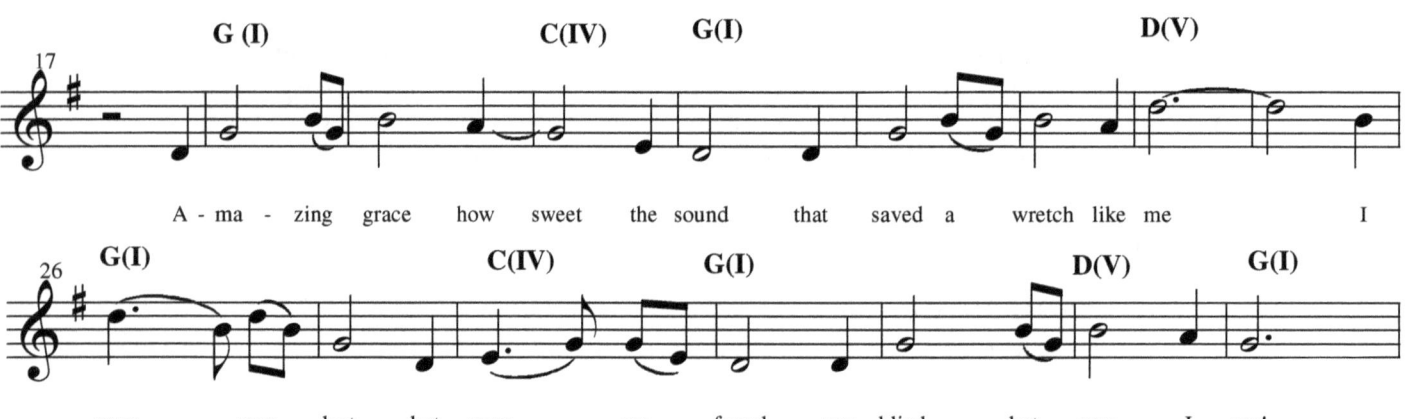

In the same way, any song can be transposed (changed from one key to another) by knowing the number progression and applying it to the desired key. You may want to transpose a song to make it easier to sing or easier to play, or to transpose up a half step or a whole step to build the dynamics.

Notice that when we transposed the chord progression we also transposed the melody line. You can assign the numbers of the scale (1-8) to the melody notes and use the scale of the new key as a reference.

# Transposition Table for All Keys

This table lists the diatonic chords in all 15 Major keys. It can be used to transpose from one key to another. Once you know the chord progression of a song and write it out in roman numerals, it is very simple to transpose the song (change it into another key) by using the same roman numeral progression with a different reference point.

For example, a I, vi, IV, V progression in the key of C Major would be C, amin, F, G. The same progression in the key of D Major would be D, bmin, G, A. In Ab it would be Ab, fmin, Db, Eb. This is very useful in raising or lowering the key of a song to make the range more singable, or for putting a song into a more "playable" key (one that is easier to finger on a certain instrument. Transposing is also a great way to take a song to a higher level dynamically.

| *Root (I)* | *ii* | *iii* | *IV* | *V* | *vi* | *vii* | *Root (I)* |
|---|---|---|---|---|---|---|---|
| C | Dmin | Emin | F | G | Amin | Bdim | C |
| C# | D#min | E#min | F# | G# | A#min | B#dim | C# |
| Db | Ebmin | Fmin | Gb | Ab | Bbmin | Cdim | Db |
| D | Emin | F#min | G | A | Bmin | C#dim | D |
| Eb | Fmin | Gmin | Ab | Bb | Cmin | Ddim | Eb |
| E | F#min | G#min | A | B | C#min | D#dim | E |
| F | Gmin | Amin | Bb | C | Dmin | Edim | F |
| F# | G#min | A#min | B | C# | D#min | E#dim | F# |
| Gb | Abmin | Bbmin | Cb | Db | Ebmin | Fdim | Gb |
| G | Amin | Bmin | C | D | Emin | F#min | G |
| Ab | Bbmin | Cmin | Db | Eb | Fmin | Gdim | Ab |
| A | Bmin | C#min | D | E | F#min | G#dim | A |
| Bb | Cmin | Dmin | Eb | F | Gmin | Adim | Bb |
| B | C#min | D#min | E | F# | G#min | A#dim | B |
| Cb | Dbmin | Ebmin | Fb | Gb | Abmin | Bbmin | Cb |

# Embellishing a Chord Progression

At times you may want to embellish a progression in a song, especially if it is as simple a progression as the one in "Amazing Grace". This is relatively easy to do using what you have already learned. Simply adding slash chords (inversions) will "pull" your ear into the next chord and give more movement to the song.

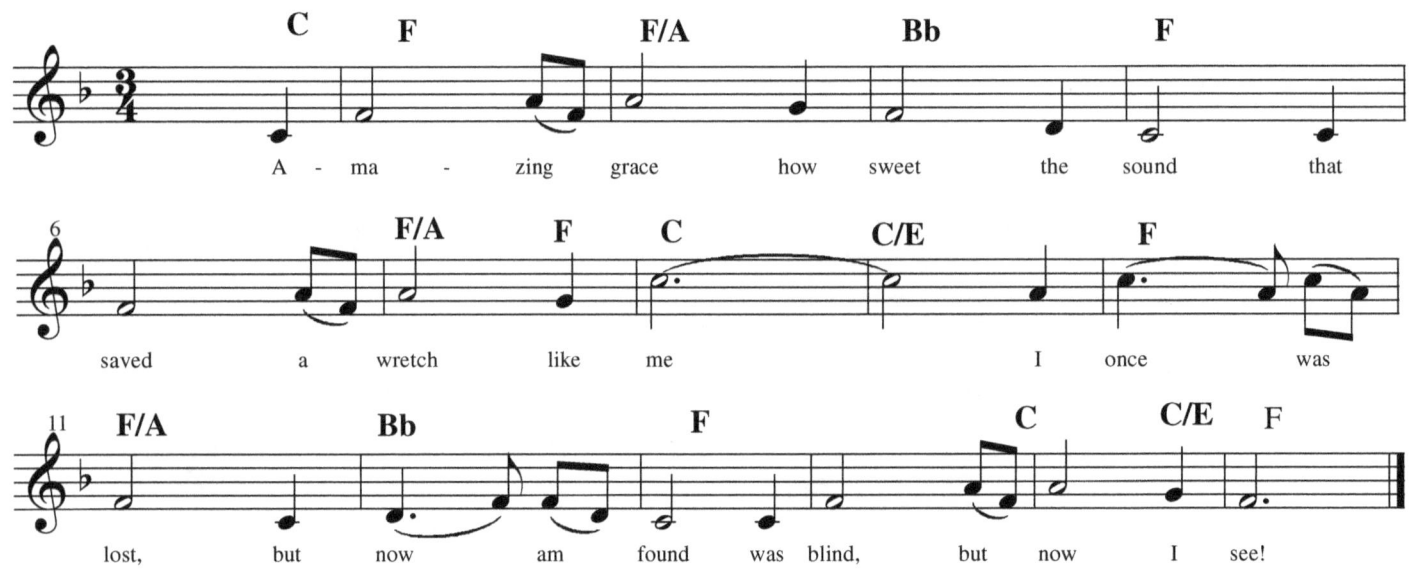

Along with the slash chords, insert some diatonic chords from the key the song is in (in this case, F major). Again, this adds a sense of movement and direction to the simple progression.

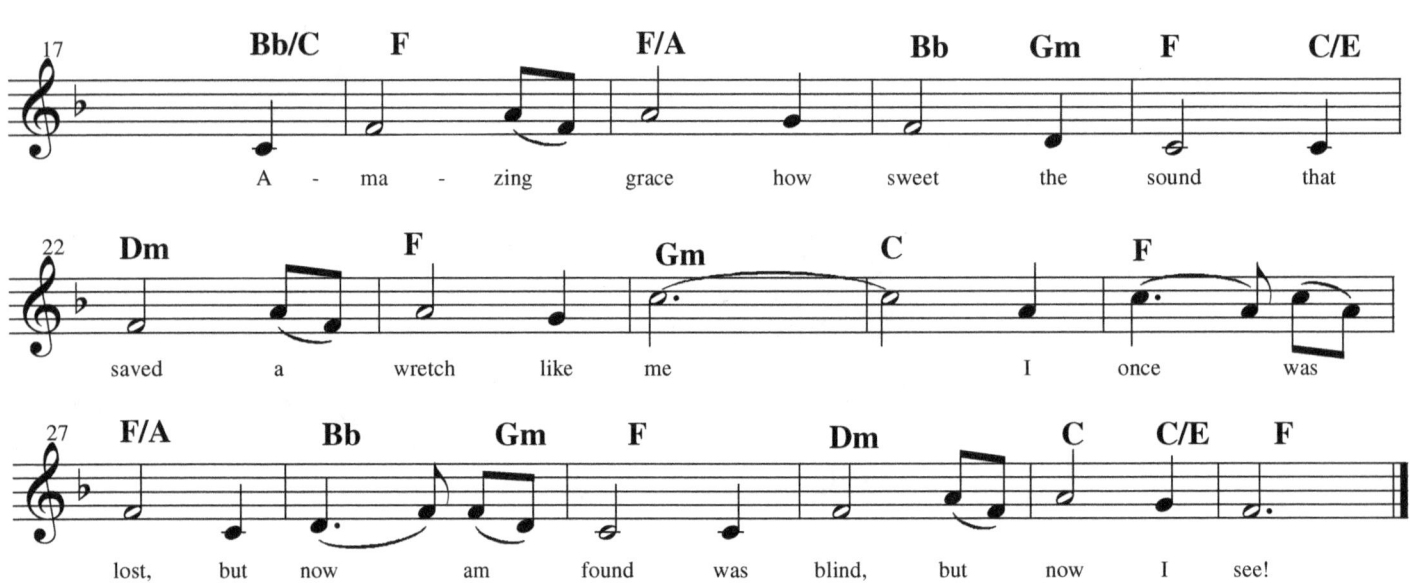

# Further Embellishment of a Progression

Here are a few more chord substitutions and embellishments that we can learn to incorporate in our songs. Remember that the basic chord progression is the same, we are merely adding to it. Also remember that any embellishments you make in one key can apply to other keys as well. Play through this chord progression and we will discuss it below.

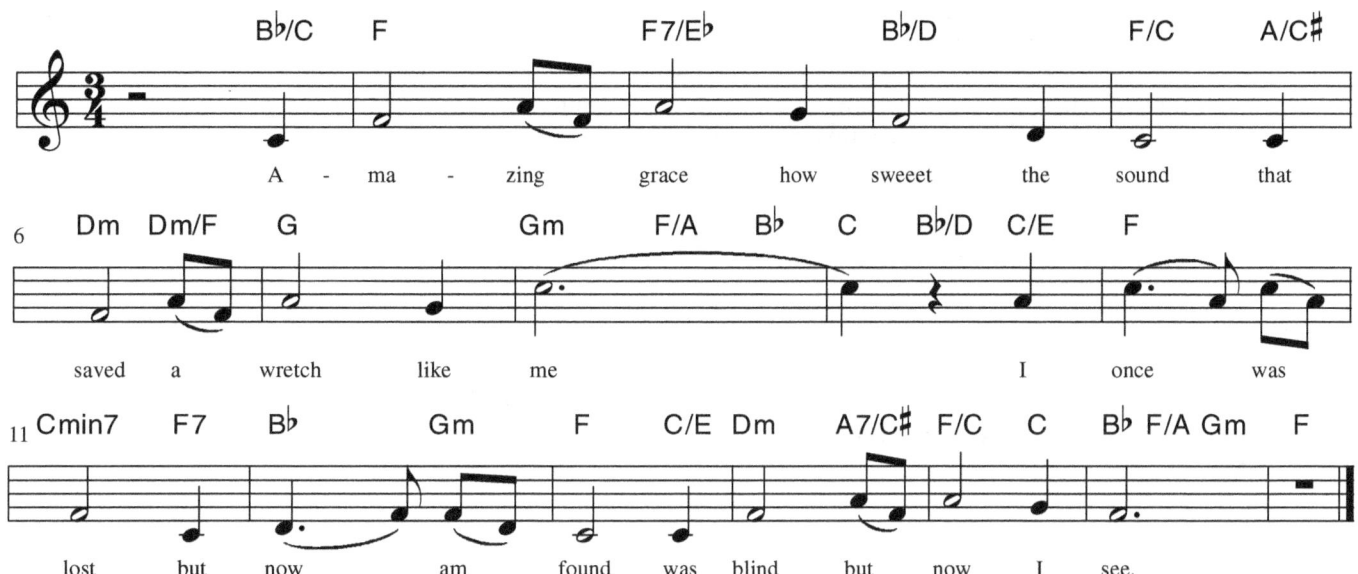

Measure 1 -- The Bb/C chord is a fully suspended 7th chord, in effect making a C chord with a b7, a 9 and an 11 added to it. Since C is the V chord of the key of F Major, this is a Dominant 7 chord, which has the effect of setting your ear up for the key chord of F.

Measures 3-4 -- The F7/Eb is a third inversion of an F7 chord. Since dominant 7th chords tend to make your ear want to hear the harmony move up a IVth (or down a Vth), this chord sets you up for the Bb or IV chord which, in this case, is a 1st inversion Bb/D, continuing the descending motion of the bass line.

Measures 5,7,11 -- Whenever you see a chord that is non-diatonic (not within the key) you may suspect that it is a SECONDARY DOMINANT. The A/C# in measure 5, the G in measure 7 and the F7 in measure 11 all include notes that are not in the key of F Major (C#, B natural and Eb, respectively). However, if you notice, each of these chords set up the following chord which is a 4th above it (A/C# sets up the Dm in measure 6, G ultimately sets up the C in measure 9, and the F7 sets up Bb in measure 12). These are called secondary dominants because they are not the V7 chord of the key, but they are the V7 chord of the chord that they preceed and they set your ear up to hear that chord.

Measures 8-9, 16 -- Diatonic walk-ups or walk-downs help to keep the harmony moving when it would otherwise have been static. Instead of a full measure of Gm, a full measure of C and a full measure of F, we walk the bass line up the major scale, incorporating diatonic chords of the key over the bass notes, filling in the empty spaces. Similarly, we walk down from IV to I (Bb to F) in measure 16.

Measures 11-12 -- The iimin -V7-I progression is a very common chord progresion. Here we use it to set up the Bb and avoid hearing two full measures of the F chord.

Measures 13-14 -- The slash chords C/E and A/C# are simply passing chords that lead your ear to the next chord.

# Rhythmic Accompaniment

One of the characteristics of a mature player is the ability to interpret a song the way it should be interpreted. Establishing the correct feel of a song is largley dependent on the rhythm patterns played by the rhythm section players. Learning what to do to rhythmically embellish a song can make you sound better than you are very quickly. Various rhythmic feels can produce straight, swing, bluesy, classical, gospel, hymn-like, contemorary and scores of other feels.

What follows are three different rhythmic interpretations of "Amazing Grace". The first is a straight quarter note feel; unimaginative and uninspiring. It works but there is no real musicality and no "life" in it. The second has more flow, more movement with the triplet arpeggios in the right hand. The third has much more personality and a bluesy feel created by the rhythms and the inversions used.

Experiment with different rhythmic feels as you play. Use your thumbs to create rhythmic patterns as you accompany. Ask yourself what the feel of the song should be within the context you are playing. Listen to good players, paying specific attention to the rhythm patterns they use and try to duplicate them. Stretch yourself by listening to types of music that you don't normally listen to in order to glean new rhythmic ideas. Practice each song with specific emphasis on the rhythmic feel you want to prioduce.

# Amazing Grace

Written in a straight quarter note three-four rhythm, to be embellished rhythmically and harmonically on the following pages.

# Rhythmic Embellishment #1
## Amazing Grace

# Rhythmic Embellishment 2

**Amazing Grace**

# Dynamic Markings, Tempo Markings and other Musical Symbols

DYNAMIC MARKINGS indicate the way in which a note or passage of music is to be played (particularly how loud or soft). TEMPO MARKINGS tell how fast or slow the music is to be played. Other musical markings help the performer to interpret the music as the composer wished it to be interpreted.

| | | | |
|---|---|---|---|
| *ff* | fortissimo -- very loud | *8va* | play the notes an octave above what is written |
| *f* | forte -- loud | *8vb* | play the notes an octave below what is written |
| *mf* | mezzo forte -- moderately loud | *accel.* | gradually become faster |
| *mp* | mezzo piano -- moderately soft | *rit.* | gradually become slower |
| *p* | piano -- soft | **Adagio** | slow |
| *pp* | pianissimo -- very soft | **Moderato** | moderate (medium) tempo |
| *sfz* | sforzando -- a sudden, strong accent | **Allegro** | fast |
| ♩= 90 | a tempo marking meaning quarter notes are at 90 beats per minute | < | gradually get louder |
| | | > | gradually get softer |

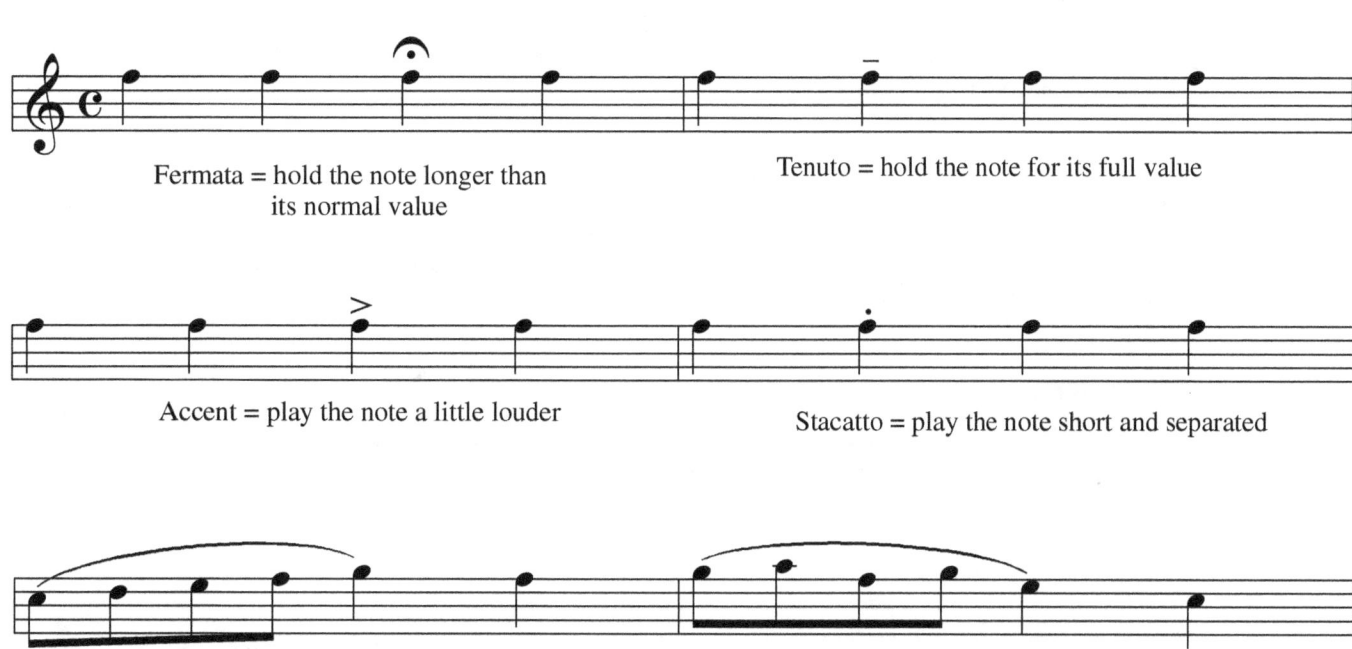

Fermata = hold the note longer than its normal value

Tenuto = hold the note for its full value

Accent = play the note a little louder

Stacatto = play the note short and separated

Slurs = play the notes legato, or smoothly and joined together, as a phrase

# Relative Minor

Every major key has a RELATIVE MINOR key that uses the same key signature. The relative minor key is a minor third (or three half steps) below it's relative major. Some songs contain one section in minor and another section in its relative major (or vice versa).

# Minor Scales

There are several minor scales. The NATURAL MINOR scale uses the key signature of its relative major scale. You can think of it as a major scale with lowered 3rd, 6th and 7th scale degrees. In the DORIAN MINOR scale the 3rd and the 7th degrees of the major scale are lowered, while in the HARMONIC MINOR scale the 3rd and the 6th degrees of the major scale are lowered. Harmonic minor is used when the V chord in your minor song is a major chord whereas the others can be used if the V chord is minor. It is beneficial to practice your natural minor scales along with your major scales, for example, play aC major scale, an A minor scale and back to a C Major scale. This helps you to mentally relate the two related scales.

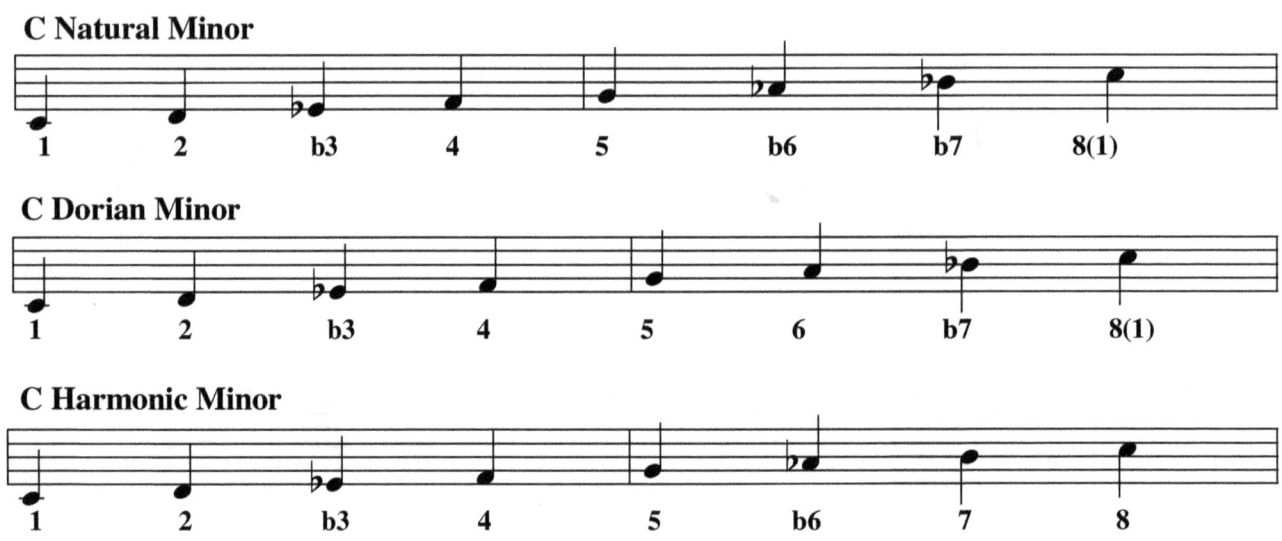

# Other Scales

The PENTATONIC SCALE is a five note scale consisting of the 1, 2, 3, 5 and 6 scale degrees of the major scale. It has many applications. It can be used to improvise over major, major seventh and dominant seventh chords. It can also be used to improvise over minor and minor seventh chords if the scale used is built from the b3rd, the 4th or the seventh note of the minor scale (For example, you may improvise over a C minor seventh chord using an Eb, an F or a Bb pentatonic scale). Each of these pentatonic scales will sound different in color over the minor chords.

C Pentatonic (two octave)

The MINOR PENTATONIC SCALE has a relative minor relationship with the pentatonic scale. That is to say, just as the natural minor scale is derived from the major scale by going down a minor third, the minor pentatonic is derived from the pentatonic by going down a minor third. In other words, a C pentatonic scale is C,D,E,G,A(1,2,3,5,6) and an A minor pentatonic scale is A,C,D,E,G (1,b3,4,5,b7).

Pentatonic chords are very common in improvising over nearly all styles of music. Practicing them in all keys and developing patterns with them will give you lots of ammunition for improvisation.

A Minor Pentatonic (two octave)

The BLUES SCALE is constructed by playing the 1, b3, 4, #4, 5, and b7 of a major scale. The lowered third and seventh scale degrees are called "blue notes" and will give your playing a decidedly "bluesy" feel.

C Blues Scale (two octave)

The DIMINISHED SCALE can be used to improvise over a diminished triad or seventh chord. It can also be played over a dominant seventh, providing lots of color tones. You want to play the diminished scale starting on the b7 or the b9 of the dominant seventh chord.

C Diminished Scale

# Possible Chord Progressions For Open Worship
(Playing/Singing in the Spirit)

We want to include times in our worship services when we play basic chord progressions and allow the people to simply and freely release their words and songs of adoration to God. It is a good idea to start simple, playing progressions that are easy to hear and follow. Then, as the congregation gets used to following, we can grow into more complex progressions.

The following progressions are suggestions that work well. Practice them in all keys (or at least in the most common keys) so that you will be able to plug them in on a moments notice (that's all the notice we get most of the time!) Also practice them with the entire band. It is also effective to use the progression of the song you just played and sing spontaneous words over it. Have fun!

| | | | | | |
|---|---|---|---|---|---|
| **I** | **Isus** | | | | |
| (G | Gsus) | | | | |
| | | | | | |
| **I** | **IV** | also | **Imaj7** | **IVmaj7** | |
| (G | C) | | (Gmaj7 | Cmaj7) | |
| | | | | | |
| **I** | **bVII** | **I** | | | |
| (G | F | G) | | | |
| | | | | | |
| **I** | **IV** | **V** | **I** | | |
| (G | C | D | G) | | |
| | | | | | |
| **I** | **ii** | **iii** | **IV** | **I** | |
| (G | Amin | Bmin | C | G) | |
| | | | | | |
| **I** | **bVI** | **bVII** | **I** | | |
| (G | Eb | F | G) | | |
| | | | | | |
| **I** | **bVII** | **IV** | **I** | | |
| (G | F | C | G) | | |
| | | | | | |
| **I** | **iv** | **I** | | | |
| (G | Cmin | G) | | | |

# Progressions for Open Worship
(Continued)

| I | IV | I/III | ii | V7 | I |
|---|----|-------|-----|-----|---|
| (G | C | G/B | Amin | D7 | G) |

| I | iii | IV | I | vi | iii | IV | V | I |
|---|-----|----|----|-----|-----|----|----|---|
| (G | Bmin | C | G | Emin | Bmin | C | D | G) |

| I | V/I | IV/I | I |
|---|-----|------|---|
| (G | D/G | C/G | G) |

| I | ii/I | V/viii | V7 | I |
|---|------|--------|-----|---|
| (G | Amin/G | D/F# | D7 | G) |

| I | II/I | viimin | iiimin |
|---|------|--------|--------|
| (G | A/G | F#min | Bmin) |

| bIII | bVII | IV | I |
|------|------|----|---|
| (Bb | F | C | G) |

| I | V/VII | vi | iii/V | IV | I/III | ii | V |
|---|-------|----|-------|----|-------|----|----|
| G | D/F# | em | bm/D | C | G/B | am | D |

| I | II/I | I | II/I | I | II/I | II | III |
|---|------|---|------|---|------|----|-----|
| G | A/G | G | A/G | G | A/G | A | B |

| imin | bVI | vmin | imin |
|------|-----|------|------|
| (Emin | C | Bmin | Emin) |

| imin | iv min | imin |
|------|--------|------|
| (Emin | Amin | Emin) |

115

# Progressions for Open Worship
## (Continued)

| imin | III | iimin | bVII | imin | |
|------|-----|-------|------|------|---|
| (emin | G | f#min | D | emin) | |

| imin | imin/bVII | bVImaj7 | ivmin | Vsus | V |
|------|-----------|---------|-------|------|---|
| (emin | emin/D | Cmaj7 | amin | Bsus | B |

| imin | bVI | ivmin | Vsus | V |
|------|-----|-------|------|---|
| (emin | C | amin | Bsus | B) |

| imin | bVII | bVI | bVII | imin |
|------|------|-----|------|------|
| emin | D | C | D | emin |

| imin | bVII | bVI | Vsus | V |
|------|------|-----|------|---|
| emin | D | C | Bsus | B |

# Improvisation

To improvise is to spontaneously create. Improvisation comes in many different packages. Many musicians and singers are intimidated by the thought of improvising. They consider it "risky" or too difficult for them to tackle. The truth is, however, that all of us improvise to one degree or another. A singer may take a liberty on the melody line of a familiar song or sing a harmony spontaneously - that is improvisation. A musician might create a chord progression or a melodic solo over a chord progression on the spur of the moment - that is improvisation. I encourage the singers and musicians in our worship teams not to be afraid of stepping out and trying new things.

Improvisation is a beautiful example of skill and anointing joined together to produce the expression of God. Improvisation is instant composition. Your goal is to play spontaneously what you hear in your head. (It is a help to many players to sing what they hear and then play it on their instruments.)

Scales, arpeggios and chords are the framework of improvisation. That is why it is so important to practice scales, arpeggios and chords in all inversions and in all keys. You cannot play what is not "under your fingers". Don't fall prey to the myth that you either have it or you don't. While improvisation may be easier for some to pick up than others, everyone can improvise if they have the determination to work at it. The longest journey begins with a single step…so let's take a step!

## Helpful hints for Basic Improvisation

- Always play with the best tone or sound possible. (Would someone want to hear sounds you are making?)
- Make phrases flow naturally. Play legato (smoothly and connected) instead of staccato (short and separated). Do this even when practicing scales and arpeggios in order to get in the habit.
- Mentally sing the phrases or runs as you play them
- Mistakes are bridges to success, so do not give up. If we all waited until we were perfect musicians before we played an instrument, there would be no music in the world.
- Experiment! Take chances! (However, I should add that practice sessions are the best place to take chances. Experimenting in worship services may not "bless" the worshipers!)
- Check out your music store for courses and play-along recordings designed to help you improvise. (Jamie Aebersold play-alongs are sold or can be ordered in many parts of the world)

# *Guidelines for Improvisation*

**WHAT TO DO:**
1) **Play the right notes** (within the key/chords in which you are playing)
2) **Play the appropriate mood** (no heavy rhythm and blues over a soft, flowing worship song)
3) **Select pretty color tones.** Sometimes the chord tones (1,3,5) sound vanilla or less than inspiring. Playing $7^{ths}$, $9^{ths}$, $11^{ths}$, and $13^{ths}$ add color and interesting texture to your chords and melodies.
4) **Develop your themes**. Most great improvisers will take a melodic or rhythmic theme and develop it. This gives continuity and a sense of direction to your solo.
5) **Build intensity.** Remember to use all of your tools to build dynamics into your solo
   - Volume (soft to loud)
   - Range (low to high)
   - Rhythm (slow to fast)
   - Harmony (single notes to chords)
   - Note choice (chord tones to color tones)
6) **Listen to good improvisers**. They greatest way to learn is to listen to great players. I don't mean casual listening, but active, critical listening. Why do I like this player? What makes their sound so inviting? What does it take to make an intense sound? A beautiful sound? A joyful sound? How can I recreate this?
7) **Listen to the message of the song and of the Holy Spirit**. Be sensitive to what the Holy Spirit is doing in the service. Play what you hear!

**WHAT NOT TO DO:**
1) **Play wrong notes** (not within the key/chords in which you are playing)
2) **Play inappropriate or unrelated melodies or rhythms**
3) **Just run the scale.** Playing the scale is not very musical sounding. Use the notes in the scale to develop patterns, phrases and musical thoughts.
4) **Don't play "words" but, rather, play musical sentences, thoughts, or phrases.**
5) **Improvise over someone else's improvisation.** ("in honor, prefer one another...")

Of course, you need to remember the basic elements of music:

1) PITCH – *What* am I saying?
   (Key, melody, chords/arpeggios, voicings/inversions, intonation)

2) RHYTHM – *When* am I saying it?
   (Time feel, groove, syncopation, periods of silence (rests), rhythmic density)

3) DYNAMICS – *How* am I saying it?
   (Loud/soft, rhythmic intensity, tension/release, accents, articulation, phrasing, legato/staccato, etc.)

# Things To Think About When Approaching A Song

## Obvious Things:

> - **Key** – Perhaps this sounds too apparent, but you'd be surprised how many players begin playing a song without the reference point of a key in their mind, hence causing many unnecessary wrong notes. Always look at your key signature!
> - **Time Signature** – Another obvious one, but you need to know it before you start.
> - **Chord Progression** – Is the chord progression simple? Repetitive? Diatonic (within the key)? Are there any non-diatonic chords in it? A little attention here will help you in memorizing the piece.
> - **Form** – Locate the sections (verse, chorus, bridge) and the phrases within these sections. Look for a specific form and look for repetition.

## Not So Obvious Things:

> - **Tempo** – This can be a real issue, especially with young or amateur bands. The tendency is to play either too fast or to allow the tempo to fluctuate. A song played at an improper tempo can lose its effectiveness and even it's sing-ability. Often a song is counted off too fast and then it speeds up even more as it unfolds. The typical places a song will speed up are when the dynamics are building (louder or more intense usually tends to get faster), during drum fills and between song sections.
>     Slow songs are generally more difficult to keep a steady tempo on because there is a longer duration between beats. Practicing with a metronome can be both eye opening and beneficial.
> - **Groove** – The "groove" is the feel of a song. The same song, same chords can be played with the same rhythms by two different bands and sound or feel very different. Something as simple as the difference between straight and syncopated can totally change a songs feel. Playing four quarter notes verses four eighth notes separated by eighth rests means the difference between a steady beat and an "in your face" punchy feel. Pay attention to the various grooves you feel in songs and try to imitate them.
> - **Chord Voicings** – For guitarists and keyboardists the chord voicing you chose can make a world of difference. Playing too many notes too low

produces a murky, muddy sound. Playing too many notes too high sounds "tinkly". Some guitarists play the bass notes of the chord too much, and they clash with the bass and the sound becomes muddy. Sometimes playing a voicing just one inversion up or down sounds altogether better (especially when keyboardists are playing organ or string sounds.) Notice the voicings you are using, experiment and play what sounds best and try to keep the voicings close when changing chords instead of jumping around playing all first position chords.

- **Dynamics Between Song Sections** – What makes a song are the dynamics. Just as it is dull and uninspiring to hear a person speak in a monotone voice, even so a song without dynamics is a lifeless, ineffective song.

    Dynamics make your song believable; as if you really mean what you are saying! When you build, really build. When you drop in intensity, drop way down. Sometimes in practice I will practice dynamics in a song to the extremes, building up to huge crescendos and then dropping off to almost silence. When you overkill dynamics in practice, they end up just about right in a worship service, because the band remembers to play them.

- **What is "My Part in the Band" on this song?** – Every instrument plays its own individual part. And sometimes each instrument plays different part in each song. The pianist who is used to playing solo normally has to incorporate aspects of the drums, the bass and the piano. When she is playing with the band, however, she must let the drummer play the drums, the bassist play the bass and she must uncomplicate her piano playing. The left hand is not always needed.

    One song may require a loud, driving, out-front electric guitar part while the next song calls for a light strumming or arpeggiating with a totally different texture. Learn to be whatever is needed.

# Working with the Team

The principles of authority and servanthood come together in a divine tension in the context of a worship team. I believe the bottom line is that *relationship* is priority to God. We are not running a business, yet there must be an authority structure if anything is to get done. We are not a putting on a show, and yet the standard needs to be as high as possible considering the talent level in the team. Establishing solid relationships within the band causes the authority structure to flow better and it creates a tighter musical sound and a sense of unity of purpose.

Notice that 2 Chronicles 5:13 says:
*"The trumpets and singers joined in unison, as with one voice, to give praise and thanks to the Lord... Then the temple of the Lord was filled with a cloud, and the priests could not perform their service because of the cloud, because the glory of the Lord filled the temple."*

***The glory of the Lord came within the context of unity.*** Contrast that with James 3:16, *"For where you have envy and selfish ambition, there you find disorder and every evil practice"*, and we see the importance of harmonious relationships. In short, we want the Lord to homogenize us relationally, spiritually and musically.

### The Leader's Responsibility

The leader is the key to instigating and maintaining this harmony within the team. It is not enough to teach on unity; the leader must model it. This is one of those attitudes that is "caught" rather than "taught". I have found that the heart of the leader rubs off on those under him. If the leader is a troublemaker, there will be trouble in the group. Conversely, is the leader has a tender, conciliatory spirit, there is generally harmony in the group.

***The leader must be a man or woman under authority.*** As we have already discussed, God's order in the tabernacle of David included a definite hierarchy. God works through channels of authority. How can I expect those under me to submit to me if I refuse to come up under those in authority over me? There is great faith, great grace and great power given to the man or woman who is under authority. The leader must have the ability to work with the pastor to bring forth the vision God has given the church. We will talk more about the worship leader/pastor relationship later.

***The leader must lead.*** He must give direction and vision, which requires him to know God's direction and have God's vision. He must also be able to communicate that vision. You don't have to be a great speaker, but you do have to have a great passion! It is important to know what you want and to be assertive enough to ask people to deliver it. Then when suggestions are made to the contrary, to lovingly and firmly stay true to the vision.

***The leader must respect every team member and honor him/her as a person.*** As leaders, we do not have the luxury of being proud, rude, jealous or overly sensitive. Remember, they are made in the image of God, they are precious and God has, in a sense, placed you as a steward over them. We will stand before God and answer for how we treated His people.

***The leader must be able to confront when necessary.*** This was one of the toughest things for me to learn. I am, by nature, a non-confronter. Unfortunately, my job requires me to confront people with the truth from time to time. I try to discern troublemakers ahead of time and weed them out before they get involved with the worship ministry. I have turned down talented players and singers because of their potentially proud or divisive attitudes. When I must confront, I keep in mind that it is for the greater good of the person I am confronting, the worship team and the body as a whole, and it is always with an eye toward restoration.

***The leader must be a servant.*** Jesus said that those in His kingdom do not lord over other people. As He came to serve, not to be served, so we must do the same. When people see our sincere hearts, motivated by love, they open up and we become effective leaders.

**The Team Member's Responsibility**

I can speak to the individual member's responsibility from the standpoint of having led many bands in many different circumstances.

***The team member I value is the one who is faithful.*** He is consistent, shows up to practices and services on time. There are few things more frustrating than having the whole team present and ready except for the one who always shows up tardy with apologies and excuses. This is disrespectful and extremely rude to those who sacrificed to be there on time. We must do what we do as unto the Lord.

***The team member I value maintains his spiritual walk.*** This one is self-explanatory, but the importance cannot be overemphasized. When our relationship with Jesus is right, we are sensitive, in tune to the Spirit, and we have something to contribute to the service. I really am not interested in mere musicians. I'm looking for some depth in God.

***The team member I value just wants to serve.*** It does not matter to her if it is up front or behind the scenes, noticed or not. She does not easily get jealous or offended if someone else is scheduled to sing this week.

***The team member I value knows his part in the band.*** A chain is only as strong as its weakest link. Each instrument, each singer, has an individual part (as we will explore later). Musically speaking, the bass needs to provide a foundation; the drummer needs keep time and provide the groove; the pianist needs to be tasteful and not too busy; the keyboardist should add support and color with different sounds, etc. When each person concentrates on their part, the sound comes together well.

***The team member I value knows the material well.*** He is free from the written music, free to worship and pay attention to the overall sound and feed off of the other musicians. The knowledge of the material also frees him up to worship!

***The team member I value follows directions well.*** She learns easily, and remembers what I tell her and does it with a good attitude.

***The team member I appreciate knows how to make suggestions at the appropriate time, with the appropriate attitude.*** A suggestion given in the right spirit can go a long way. A "word fitly spoken" is a wonderful thing. By contrast, a word unfitly spoken is an awkward, uncomfortable thing. Sometimes, for time's sake, or for simplicity's sake, or for reasons that I know and no one else does, I need to disregard or postpone a suggestion. Having a team member that understands that is a great asset.

# Practical Issues
## Simple Ideas That Might Help

This section is sort of a topic pool of ideas to make the process of building a healthy worship team easier. These ideas come from experience, foolish mistakes, trial and error, common sense and divine wisdom. They are by no means covered exhaustively nor do I claim to have all wisdom on the subjects. God may give you other insight in these areas as they apply to your unique situation, but, for what its worth, here are a few approaches that might help you.

**Choosing band members**

Choosing the right worship personnel is crucial. It is much easier to "lay hands on" people than to "lay hands off" them (that is, easier to ask them to join than to ask them to step down). Some forethought is helpful. At times I have, out of desperation and the need to fill a spot, asked somebody to join the team and later found out that they weren't solid, did not last long, or worse, caused trouble in the team. It would have been better to be patient and wait for the right person. Preventive maintenance is better than crisis control.

Prayerfully consider the way to build your team. In recruiting members, I usually put a spot in our church bulletin that say something like:

"*If you consider yourself a worshiper, have been attending our church for at least one year, can play or sing well, and believe the worship ministry is for you, please contact...*"

This type of announcement seems to weed out the "casual inquirer". I word it that way because this is exactly what I want. ***I want worshipers***, not just players and singers. ***I want committed people.*** They should be committed first of all to Jesus, then to the body of believers whom they will be serving, then to the team itself. I require all new worship team members to go through the process of becoming official members of the church. I don't believe a person should be allowed to minister to a body of believers to whom they are not committed enough to become an official member. We will all stand before God some day and give an account of how we have served these people. It is serious business. Finally, ***I want people who are competent in their gifting***, people who want to strive for excellence.

Then I hold auditions. I ask questions along the lines of those three things I want in a team member. If they are not up to the standard musically or vocally, I encourage them, if they still feel a desire for this ministry, to take lessons for a year and come back and try again. I give them the name and number of an instructor and bless them as they try. If they are potential team members, I give them a copy of our goals and expectations (so that we are all on the same page) and I invite them to a practice to see how well they fit in. I usually allow them to practice for a while (4 to 6 weeks) before they minister in a service. This helps to break the ice a bit.

Sometimes you don't get the luxury of hand picking your own team members. Working with a team that is already in place can be good news or bad news. It can be great because there is already a chemistry between the members and they have experience in playing together. It can be bad because they may be stuck in a rut, have questionable ability or commitment levels, or they may have a totally different vision for worship than you do.

The first time I was ever put in charge of an existing band was a great learning experience for me. I was a new kid on the block, dealing with an established band with an established style, and I was younger than most of them. The process of change was painful. I had to pray, confront, raise the bar and call the band to a higher standard, and sometimes lovingly rebuke. Some left the band. But God added others, and worship went to a higher level. My best advice to someone in that position is: operate under the authority of the church leadership, establish a vision and remain true to it, and try to be a reconciler in all situations.

I do realize that we all have to work with what we have. Sometimes building an excellent team out of the raw material that we have is a bit like trying to make a silk purse out of a sow's ear. But with God, all things are possible! He knows our hearts and He will bless our efforts. If you do not have the right personnel, pray them in. In short, here's the kind of people I pray for and try to choose:

> Choose worshipers
> Choose committed people
> Choose people of integrity
> Choose competent musicians
> Choose faithful people
> Choose people with servants hearts
> Choose those who understand and will get behind the vision of your church leadership.

**Running a Practice**

I am beginning to view practices as wonderful time of opportunity to be seized instead of necessary evils to be endured. They are a great chance to impart vision; blend together musically, socially and spiritually; teach; iron out problems; pray for each other's needs; learn how to worship; and, oh yeah, go over some songs.

I must first say that which goes without saying: If you do not practice, you will sound like you did not practice. I have been in churches that met a few minutes before the service to hash out a list of songs. Without exception they all sounded like they didn't practice. Perhaps professionals can do that but most churches aren't dealing with professionals. A separate practice is necessary.

The first thing a practice needs is a leader. There are few things worse than a floundering, aimless practice with eight or ten people, all with different ideas, trying to implement them. The worship leader must know what he wants and know how to communicate that to others.

I have found that the key here is preparation. If I have spent adequate time preparing the song lists, joining together medleys, paying attention to keys and key changes, intros, outros and interludes, the dynamics and flow of each song and the set as a whole, what I hear each instrument doing in each song, melodies and harmonies, etc., then practice goes much smoother. Then I can concentrate on the relational aspects of the practice. I can entertain suggestions and compare them to what I am already thinking a song should be. I can be assertive when I need to be and ask for what I want in confidence and in a humble spirit.

There are a few elements I try to have at all practices. One is a relational dynamic. We need time to unwind from the cares of the day and feel comfortable with each other. Small talk and humor are absolute necessities. We also spend time in prayer at practice. It sets our minds on Jesus and focuses our hearts on Him, His purposes and on the people to whom we will be ministering. We also pray for one another's needs, strengthening that relational bond. At times I will do a short (5-10 minute) teaching on something the Lord laid on my heart as a focus of worship that week or about an aspect of God that is mentioned in a song we are doing this week.

Another novel idea is to actually practice worshiping at our practices! It is very easy to focus so much on musical or technical aspects that we forget to worship. Some of the most powerful times of worship I've ever experienced were at a practice session. Sometimes God will quicken to us a theme that He wants to communicate in the worship service. In the end, if we simply run through the songs at practice, we tend to do the same on Sunday during the service.

Practices should be the place where there is freedom to take chances, try new things and make mistakes. Singers should take advantage of practices to solidify harmony parts and memorize the words so as not to be staring at a piece of paper on Sunday morning. It is also helpful to have a sound man at practice to set the monitor levels and mix the house speakers.

Practice is a profitable time to gel as a team. Take advantage of it!


**Making a Songlist**
There are many things to consider when choosing songs for a worship service. Here are a few suggestions:
- ➢ **Don't forget the One you are worshiping!** As I related earlier, I was rightly rebuked by as elderly member of our congregation years ago because it was 25 minutes into the song service before the name of Jesus was mentioned. Remember that in Revelation 5, it is the Lamb is the One who is in the midst of the throne, in the midst of the elders, in the midst of the creatures and the throng of the redeemed. Jesus, the Lamb, must be central to our songs.
- ➢ **Don't get into a rut.** There is no cut and dry formula for organizing a songlist. My nature is to be administrative and organized, so I usually "plan my work and work my plan." This can, however be detrimental to what our awesome, interactive God wants to do at a given time. It is very important to be sensitive and rely on the leading of the Holy Spirit.

    I usually start with faster songs because it draws the congregation together and tends to jump start them as they make the transition from the cares of the world to the presence of God. But sometimes a slow song is just the thing to gently bring the people in. Worship tends to flow into a more intimate atmosphere as a service unfolds, so I usually end with slower songs. Yet, there are times when a fast song "seals the deal", and puts an exclamation point on what God has been speaking during the worship time. The bottom line is, be flexible and be open.

- **Stay under your covering of authority.** I have worked with pastors that had a different philosophy of worship than I did. This is not always easy, but it usually is a learning experience. There is a time to make a godly appeal. There is also a time to realize that the pastor has the burden, the vision and the responsibility before God to lead that church. If you disagree with him, approach him respectively. In the end we are there to support him in his role. Your motto should be: "communicate and cooperate."

- **Be spontaneous.** Work with your band and your singers to learn how to be spontaneous within a service. God can lead you as you make your list and that list might be perfect for that occasion. But God can also lead you on the spur of the moment. There have been times when the songs I picked weren't working at all. It seemed that the Lord wanted to speak something else. As we were sensitive and changed direction, adding a song we hadn't planned to do the Spirit of God confirmed and moved mightily.

    As a word of caution, we also want to guard against the opposite extreme, which is planning nothing and waiting around to see if the Lord speaks anything. That can potentially be a vacuum from which confusion reigns. Someone needs to lead the worship. That leader needs to be led by God.

- **Pick songs that say something.** I guess it's the teacher in me, but I can't stand songs that say nothing. The church has too long been plagued with melodies filled with fluff and no meat. I love some of the old hymns because they contain weighty theology in a palatable form.

    Some songs either have very little of substance to say or are altogether theologically incorrect their message. We sang the old song "Blow the trumpet in Zion" for years as a joyful, dancing song. Then we realized that the context that scripture comes from has to do with repentance, sackcloth, ashes and a solemn assembly! What were we doing!? I challenge you to use songs that contain the deep, penetrating message of the gospel.

- **What is the Lord speaking to your church in that season?** If it is a season of victory, wear out the victory songs. If God is challenging your congregation to stretch their faith, pour on the faith songs. I am a firm believer that a word fitly spoken and a song fitly sung are equally effective.

- **Be sensitive to your context and your congregation.** Some songs will work in certain contexts and not in others. Congregations worship in different ways. What will work in one part of the country (or other countries) isn't guaranteed to be effective in truly bringing your people into worship. The church I attend presently has two Sunday morning services and a Sunday evening service. All three services are very different because the makeup of the congregation is different. What brings one group of people into a heartfelt, deep encounter with God is may hardly move another. Our job is to use the gift of wisdom that Jesus gives us and do whatever it takes to bring those we serve into true worship.

*Worship is not about what we like,
it's about Who we love.*

- **Sing to the Lord, not just about Him.** Make it personal. Sing in first person. Try this little test and see if you do not find the same results that I have found: the next time you do a song in third person (referring to God as Him or He) change the lyrics around to first person (referring to God as You). You will see a greater intensity as the people sing personally to a personal God.
- **Remember, it is not about you.** I have learned that worship is not about what I like, it's about Who I love. I sometimes am compelled to play songs that I do not particularly care for simply because they work… they bring the congregation into worship, and that blesses the people and it blesses God. Isn't that what we are here for?

**Working with Singers**

Incorporating singers into the praise team has obvious benefits and many possible pitfalls.

A singer should think of his or her voice as their instrument. They are not just singing, but they are making music with their voice. I have found that most singers don't see themselves as "musicians". They need to think musically. They need to apply themselves to a certain amount of practicing of vocal technique, as other instrumentalists should, to increase their talent. They should feel free to improvise at the appropriate times within the boundaries set forth for them. Perhaps most importantly, they need to think and function as a part of the overall band. Their part needs to blend, not stick out.

Choosing singers for a worship team is not much different than choosing instrumentalists, with the possible exception that any *flaws in character tend to be magnified in this particular office.* A self-focused, showy singer can quench the Spirit of God very quickly. The mindset of the world is so opposite from the mindset of a true worshiper. Brokenness is what is needed here. I have shunned people who were naturally more talented, yet not broken, in favor of others who were not as skillful, but much more humble and transparent.

If you have more than one singer, you have to deal with the issue of whether everyone will sing unison or whether harmony parts will be assigned. In any singing group, boisterous voices that don't blend or that sing with wide, sweeping vibrato are to be avoided. Sometimes the wonderful soloist doesn't make a very good group singer. They have to learn how to homogenize with a group.

Depending on the personnel you have, you will want to approach harmony from one of two different angles. If your group can read music well or is used to singing in a choral ensemble with written music, you may want to write parts out for them and assign them according to range. This takes some time, but it can work very well because when they learn their parts they usually have them for good and don't switch parts in the middle of a song. If your group does not read music well, but has the ability to hear parts naturally, it is possible to "turn them loose" and let them find their own harmonies. Sometimes they need a little help ironing out a few parts and at times they may need to be made aware when they inadvertently switch parts in a song, doubling one part and leaving another unsung. But, all this aside, this can also work very well and save you the time of writing and rehearsing parts.

Above all, singers need to be worshipers. They should memorize their parts and the words to the songs as much as is possible, so as to free themselves up to look away from the page and look unto Jesus. I would encourage singers to seek vocal instruction from a competent teacher (preferably one who understands the worship dynamic) and to invest in vocal workout tapes which are available at many Christian bookstores.


**Incorporating the Choir**

For many years I was the worship leader at a church that had more than enough people to maintain a good sized choir, yet we didn't. There were several reasons. One reason was the old standby, "We've never done that around here before." Another, to be honest, was that I was leery of what would happen if we started one. That is a lot of people to deal with, a lot of work writing parts (most of the songs we sang had no commercial parts written for them), a lot of hours practicing and what I considered could be a lot of logistical nightmares. Besides that, we did not want just a singing choir… we wanted a worshiping choir. Could I stock this choir with the right kind of people who had a heart and vision for worship?

Well, at the exhortation of my pastor, I did start one and the benefits have far outweighed the cost. The choir is an incredible boost to the dynamic level of our worship services. The intensity level is much higher, the congregation participates more, we are making room for the gifts of singing that had gone without a place to be exercised until now, and the people in the choir feel much more attached to the body as a whole.

To anyone contemplating beginning a worship choir I would give these words of advice:

1) **Choose worshipers.** No choir is better than a dead choir. We need hearts on fire and voices that can carry a tune.
2) **Start slowly and build strong.** It is not a bad idea to practice several months before singing in an actual worship service. Get to know each other, get comfortable with each other, gel together, and sound good before your first public appearance. Then only have the choir once a month or every other week for a while. Slowly work into every week.
3) **Be open minded.** You would be surprised who can sing well enough to contribute to a choir.
4) **The choir does not have to sing on every part of every song.** It is quite effective when they are out for a verse and in on the chorus, or when they sing melody on the verse and burst into harmony on the chorus.
5) **Don't be afraid to stretch them.** It's amazing what ordinary people can do when you believe in them. In preparing for a series of special meetings our

choir once learned twenty-one challenging songs in five practice sessions. They weren't sure that they could do it but they did and they did a wonderful job.

**Raising up leaders**

Through the years one of the most common problems I have encountered in working with other churches is the lack of vision regarding training leaders in the worship ministry. We are to be about the business of making disciples, and that includes working together to raise up potential worshipers within our congregations. I have known churches that have neglected this area and when their worship leader moved away, the congregation suffered because there was no one to take over.

I believe that a very important part of my job is to recognize those with a gift of worship around me and to work towards training them and releasing them into ministry. If God ever calls me somewhere else, I want the worship ministry to continue on as good or better than it was when I was here. We need to be actively pursuing those around us with potential gifts.

This, of course, means that we cannot hold on too tightly to our positions of ministry. We have to step aside and allow others room to learn, grow, make mistakes and mature in their giftings. Here are a few things to consider if you recognize someone with a gift of worship:

- Watch them for a while. Notice their walk, their passion for the Lord and their musical giftings. Remember to "lay hands on no man suddenly".
- Pray about their place in the worship ministry and about God's timing for them.
- If possible, "try them out" in a position of lower visibility, such as leading worship for small groups or youth meetings. Are they faithful?
- Take them under your wing. Encourage their strengths and help them in their weaknesses. Work with them musically and spiritually. Spend time with them and impart your heart for worship to them.
- Call them up higher. Give them a vision for being set apart to this ministry to the Lord.
- Don't try to make a "worship clone" out of them. Set them free to be themselves within the boundaries you set for them. Different is good.
- Try this method of gradually releasing them into ministry:
    1) I do, you watch
    2) I do, you help
    3) You do, I help
    4) You do, I watch

In the end, you will be glad you invested the time in them. Your load will be lighter and your congregation will be blessed by the diversity that God has given you through the various members of your body.

# The Rhythm Section

The rhythm section of the band generally consists of any combination of the following instruments: drums, bass, piano/keyboard, rhythm guitar, percussion. These instruments create the foundation of a song and sustain the rhythmic and harmonic support for other instrumentalists and/or singers. If the rhythm section is together, the song sounds tight, solid and sure. If the rhythm section is not together, the song is unsure and does not communicate well, and can, in fact, be very distracting to worship.

As a rule the rhythm section wants to:
1) **Be a rhythmic and harmonic foundation from which the song flows.** Although the rhythm instruments can also provide color, they primarily want to define the tune in terms of the harmony (chords played) and the rhythm time feel). The old adage, "less is more" fits here. The simpler you can keep it, the tighter it sounds. Many immature musicians want to play too much and too often and end up crowding or cluttering the sound.
2) **Capture the mood of the song.** There are so many different moods and styles in praise and worship music. It takes a maturity to do all of them well. With immature players every song tends to sound alike. A seasoned band will approach each song individually and interpret it in such a way as to communicate the message effectively. They "speak" with the music the same thing that the lyrics are saying. They create an atmosphere conducive to worship.
3) **Play tightly together.** The tempo needs to be proper and steady. Each instrument needs to have a feel for where the down beats are, hit syncopated punches together, start, stop, modulate and transition between song sections together. One of the primary ways to produce a "tight" sound is for the bass guitar to attack its notes in the same rhythms as the bass drum. If a band works especially hard on intros, interludes and endings the rest of the sections tend to take care of themselves and the overall sound is tight.
4) **Enhance, not interfere.** Do not override the vocals or other instruments. Be your part of the band, but listen to the overall sound, not just your sound.

**Perhaps it would be helpful to briefly discuss the role of each instrument in the rhythm section.**

## *Drums*

Perhaps I run the risk of stating the obvious when I say that a drummer's job is to keep time. Unfortunately, many drummers lose sight of that fact and, in the face of all the fills, complicated bass drum patterns, syncopated punches and other "musicality", time takes a back seat. Don't try to sound cool; try to make the band sound tight. You and the bass guitar are the two most important instruments when it comes to creating a tight sound. When you are together, it is *good*. When you are not together, it is *real bad!* Become best buddies and learn to play well together. Your congregation will rise up and call you blessed!

A good drummer punctuates a song by using dynamics to communicate emotion. A good drummer make s song "feel" great, but doesn't stick out, or draw attention to himself in the process. A good drummer understands that he doesn't have to play every measure of every song. A great drummer listens to the worship leader and follows him.

Here are a few things for drummers to consider:
- Compliment, don't clutter
- Practice with a metronome (It does wonders for your pride!)
- Take some lessons: learn how to count; learn to play in different time signatures; learn proper technique
- Make time your priority and then add color
- Watch your drum rolls, fills and between sections (verse to chorus, chorus to bridge, etc.). Many times this is where tempo is lost
- Keep your bass drum and the bass guitar together. This makes a tight sound.
- Pay attention to dynamics. You can make or break a song by how you build and fade
- Try doing a five-minute cymbal solo using different rhythms, tempos, and dynamic intensities. (Five minutes is a long time!). This helps to build creativity and "musicality" into your playing.
- Listen carefully to good drummers: What makes them sound good? Try to copy what they do. It can only enhance your skill.
- Tune your drum heads, or get someone who knows what they are doing to tune them. Play with the best sound you can get.


### *Bass*

The bass is my favorite instrument to play, perhaps because it is akin to my personality and gifting. The bass is behind the scenes, yet it holds things together. It gives a solid foundation, contributes to both the harmonic and rhythmic structure of the song, and is crucial to the tightness of the sound. It is seldom noticed by the average person in the congregation, yet would be sorely missed if it wasn't there.

A good bass player is tight with the drums. A good bass player pays attention to the rhythm, duration and articulation of his notes, for that is where the groove comes from. A good bass player plays the notes right on the beats before he worries about walks or fills.

Here are a few things for bassists to consider:
- Be the foundation
- Pay attention to your tone. A soft round tone is usually better for slower tunes, while a brighter tone works well for lively tunes. Adjust your equalization and your right hand position up and down the body to get different tones. (Brighter toward the back bridge, rounder toward the neck)

- Experiment with scales, walks and fills, but be careful not to play too much and lose your "foundation"
- Explore the upper register but, as a rule, stay down lower
- Pay attention to articulation. Breathe out your notes on slow tunes. Punch the faster, brighter ones. Play what you play as though you meant to play it that way.
- As you change register (down the strings, up the neck), your volume varies. Try to remain consistent in your volume.
- Take lessons. Learn scales and arpeggios in different positions. Learn right and left hand technique.

## *Rhythm Guitar*

Rhythm guitar differs from lead guitar in that it is mainly occupied with strumming and picking chords in time. The important thing for rhythm guitarists to remember is that rhythm guitar is *rhythm* guitar. Rhythm is its first name for a good reason. Rhythm is the most important thing for a rhythm guitarist. You are part of the rhythm section and your job is to establish and keep a consistent tempo. The right chords at the wrong time is wrong. The wrong chords at the right time is also wrong. You have to play the right chords and you have to play them at the right tempo. Again, perhaps this sounds like stating the obvious, but it has become obvious to me over the years that this is just what rhythm guitarists need to hear.

A good rhythm guitarist has a good sense of time. He plays solid and distinct chords. He helps to supply a solid foundation for the other players.

Here are a few things for rhythm guitarists to consider:
- Practice with a metronome. Pay attention to time.
- Take lessons. Learn different strumming and picking techniques.
- You do not have to play all the time
- Don't get into a rut. Some guitarists have only one strumming pattern. They play the right chords, but it doesn't sound like the song.
- You can break some songs up by picking the verse and strumming the chorus
- Try different chord inversions and positions. Do not hammer on the bass strings. Play the full chord and let the bass guitar play bass.

## *Piano/ Keyboard*

The piano and the keyboard are parts of the rhythm section that are complex in their contribution. A pianist incorporates rhythm, harmony and melody as well as a wide range of dynamic expression. These instruments can easily do solo worship because the keyboardist can be the drummer, the bass, the harmony and the melody if necessary. This versatility can be a real asset of one is playing solo. However, it can also be a stumbling block within the context of a band. I teach my piano students to play solo, and to play in a band, and the two are quite different.

A good pianist lets the drums provide the beat and the bass provide the bass notes. A good pianist plays the chord progression using smooth sounding voicings. A good pianist can fill holes with tasteful fills, yet not step on others or be too busy.

If you are playing an electronic keyboard, sounds and textures are variables you must think about. A good keyboardist can set the mood of a piece and add color by using the right sound. Strings or pad sounds are great to create a full sound. Nothing beats a good Hammond organ sound on songs where it is appropriate. Even horn sounds can work well, providing the horn sound on your keyboard does not sound too cheesy or fake. A good keyboardist has an imagination and a good ear to be able to hear what would fit well in a given song.

Here are a few things for pianists/ keyboardists to consider:
- When playing solo, think of the patterns that the drummer would play on the song and incorporate them into your playing. Think sub-divided beats (eighth and sixteenth notes) and use your thumbs to hammer out the subdivisions.
- Also when playing solo, use your left hand to create the bass feel. Use inversions (slash chords) to give the progression a feel of moving smoothly. Don't play all the chords in root position. Using inversions can make you sound much better than you are!
- When playing with a band, do not overuse your left hand. You could be playing a different rhythm (or even a different bass note) than the bass player and therefore cluttering the sound.
- Play interesting and pleasant sounding voicings. The 1,1,3,5 and 1,7,3,5 voicings (see the section on *"Voicing Triads and Seventh Chords"*) give a nice sound without being too crowded. You can also add color tones ($7^{th}$, $9^{th}$ $11^{th}$ $13^{th}$) to these voicings.
- Listen to the overall sound of the band. Is what you are playing complimenting or complicating that sound? With many players there is a tendency to play too much.
- Practice using scales and arpeggios to create fills in dead spaces (but be sensitive not to play on top of other players that might be doing the same thing)
- Play what you do play like you mean it. Some pianists play so softly that they can not be heard and they end up making no real contribution to the band.

## *Lead Guitar*

Many times the person playing the electric guitar will be concerned with the same things mentioned under rhythm guitar. If you have both a rhythm (acoustic) and a lead or electric guitar, we want to make sure they are not always doing the same thing. If the lead player is constantly strumming chords, he is missing out on contributing color to the sound.

A good lead player does not play lead all the time. If he does solos, it is sparingly and tastefully. A few good solos are better than "noodling" all the time. A good lead player thinks in terms of textures, color, and rhythmic and harmonic enhancement. He doesn't play on top of everybody all the time. He is considerate of the overall sound.

Here are a few things for lead guitar players to consider:
- Don't feel like you have to play all the time.
- Memorize the chord progressions .
- Use effects pedals, volume swells, and tone to add color to the overall sound.
- Don't get stuck in a rut playing the same old lead licks. Consider taking lessons from someone who plays a different style from you. Incorporate different styles into your playing.
- Listen to great worship guitarists. Listen to different styles of guitarists than you normally listen to. Pay attention, ask questions and learn from them.
- Try different things in different songs: shank patterns, single note rhythmic patterns, simple arpeggios.
- When you solo, think melodically. Try to build the dynamics of your solo.
- Look over the section on "*Improvisation*".
- Practice playing with recordings.
- Make sure your guitar is in tune.

## *Percussionists*

The use of percussion in worship is becoming more popular, and for a good reason. Percussion is a wonderful way to add color, texture and interesting rhythmic feels to songs. The use of congas, bongos, tambourines, shakers, cabasa, djemba (African drum), triangles, chimes and other percussion instruments can add lots of depth and maturity to your sound.

A good percussionist is versatile. He does not play the same instrument or same rhythmic pattern on every song. A good percussionist has a good sense of time. You must be able to keep a good, steady tempo. A good percussionist thinks in terms of complimenting the overall sound. He doesn't stick out above the rest of the band. He is like a good seasoning. The right amount makes the taste of the food it is used on better, but if you use too much, it ruins the taste.

Here are a few things for the percussionist to consider:
- Put a premium on tempo and rhythmic feel. Practicing with a metronome is a great way to become consistent with your tempo.
- Listen to recordings that include great percussionists. Pay attention to what they are doing and where they do it.
- Listen to the overall sound of the band and notice how your volume level and intensity fit in with the others. Adjust to what fits.
- Remember that, like other color instruments, you don't necessarily have to play all the time, or play loud all the time. Sometimes one little "ding" on the triangle is the perfect touch in a song. Be flexible.
- Play the appropriate emotional feel for each song. Some loud, boisterous Latin patterns create wonderful, energetic grooves. Other times a quite shaker is the perfect touch. Say what the song says.

> Try to purchase quality percussion products. Some are cheap and they sound that way. Tune the heads on your drums to allow for a good tone.

## *Wind and Brass Instruments*

These are two other groups of instruments that can add a wonderful expressiveness to worship. Flutes, clarinets, saxophones, trumpets, trombones, etc. can be great assets.

One problem is that most players of these instruments learned how to play in high school bands and have very little experience in improvisation. They *read* well but they do not "*flow*" well. They need to have parts written for them. That means that the worship leader (or someone to whom he delegates the task) needs to know how to write and transpose the parts to the appropriate key for each instrument. Sometimes worship leaders feel insufficient for this task, but I have known some that, given enough encouragement and a little knowledge, have risen to the task and done well.

If you have players of these instruments that *can* improvise, thank the Lord your God from whom every good gift flows! I have seen groups of horn players that can sit around and compose their own parts during a practice. They play well together and enhance the sound tremendously. I have worked with flute players that play with beautiful tones who can improvise on call. Turn these people lose and let their gifts bless the body!

Here are a few things for wind and brass players to consider:
> Watch your intonation. The correct part played out of tune sounds bad.
> Play with the best tone possible at all times.
> Be expressive. The right notes at the right time with no expression is flat and dull.
> As with the other instruments, listen to recordings of good players of your own kind. Pay attention to the blend, the dynamics and the overall sound that a good horn section produces. How do they achieve that sound?
> Do not play all the time. The reason the flute sounds so well in this song is that it was not there in the last song. There is no need to play the melody to every song. Play counter-melodies or written parts. Play the melody sometimes, but please, please, not all the time.

## Getting Better

If we would be great, we must be taught. The Word of God exhorts us to do what we do with all of our heart, as unto the Lord. We learned in earlier chapters the importance if skill in worship. An ever-growing knowledge of music theory and of your instrument is needed to offer the Lord what He is worthy of.

### Practicing

There are many ways to better yourself, but they all begin by making up your mind and disciplining yourself to the task. A regular practice routine is the best way to consistently grow on your instrument. Scales, arpeggios, chord progressions, inversions, interpretation of different styles, play-along with recordings, etc. all can be utilized to build a fruitful practice time. I tell my music students that consistency is the key. It is better to do fifty sit ups a day than to skip a week and then do 500. All that gets you is sore muscles! Likewise it is better to practice a shorter period of time, but more consistently. Practice with purpose. What are you trying to accomplish? Have a goal and move toward it.

**Private lessons**

The musicians in the Old Testament were said to be "under the hands of" their instructors. This is a beautiful phrase creating the word picture of a "hands on" molding of ones gift by another who is more skillful.

More than likely there are good instructors on your instrument in your area. Take the time to seek them out and begin taking private lessons. It is great if your can find a Christian who is sympathetic to your "style" of music, but the basics of your instrument can be learned from anyone who is knowledgeable. If you can not find a good professional teacher, seek to learn from anyone who is better than you. Grab a friend and let him show you some stuff. Do whatever you can to grow!

**Instructional Videos**

There are good instructional videos available for many instruments. Some will not be very helpful because they are aimed at a specific idiom of music, but you can gleam something from most of them. Make use of them. If you cannot find one for your particular instrument, find a good live praise and worship video that has someone playing your instrument on it and watch what they are doing.

**Listening**

I have mentioned listening several times. I tell my students that if they learn how to listen right they can learn more from recordings of great players than they can from me. By listening I do not mean just casually listening (like background music while you wash the dishes,) but I mean hard, critical listening and asking lots of questions. What is this musician doing that I like so well? How does he play the notes and chords? How does he play the rhythmic feel of this song. The beautiful phrasing of the improvisation, how is he playing it? What scale is he using? How does the way he approaches this song differ from the way he approaches other songs? Active listening and lots of questions are priceless when it comes to learning your instrument. It really is the greatest way to learn.

# Practical Tips for Prophetic Worship

We have already discussed the fact that as we worship, God releases a prophetic anointing, opening the door for His particular word for a particular people to come forth. This section will focus of the practical aspects of that process. How do we learn to flow in the prophetic and introduce this to our worship team and to our congregation?

**What is prophecy?**
It is always beneficial to know why you do what you do. What is the purpose and function of prophecy as a gift of God? Why should we, as Paul tells us, especially desire the gift of prophecy (1 Cor.14:1)?

Revelation 19:10 says: *"Worship God! For the testimony of Jesus is the Spirit of prophecy."* This passage implies that there is a correlation between worship, the testimony of Jesus and prophecy. True prophecy will always be a "testimony of Jesus." Paul also tells us that those who prophesy strengthen, encourage and comfort the hearers. This is the reason why God wants this gift to operate in the church.

**How does it come forth?**
A good first step in introducing your body to prophetic worship is teaching about it. I have found that when people see the overwhelming number of scriptural references concerning music, worship and prophecy they are generally very open to it. A little knowledge goes long way. Set aside an evening or a Saturday and get your team together to study the scriptures and discuss the direction God may want to go in this area.

The prerequisite to communicating God's word to others is to first hear it for your self. We have to be open and available for Him to speak to us. Seek God through the week. Train yourself to hear His voice. Sometimes He will speak a specific theme for a service. Sometimes the theme will be for a longer period of time - a season the body is going through. At times I make a song list based on what I feel the Lord is speaking that week. Other times I am into the actual service before a "theme" becomes clear.

There are several ways that a prophetic word might come forth. It can, of course, be spoken forth. It can be sung spontaneously, that is, a brand new song composed on the spur of the moment. It can also be a song that is already composed and says precisely what the mind of the Lord is at the moment. I remember one service years ago that seemed to never get off the ground. We never reached a high level of worship until we sang a certain song, an old hymn that spoke of God's faithfulness. Suddenly, a great roar of praise burst forth from the collective heart of the congregation. This was what the Lord was speaking that morning. Nothing else would bring the congregation so deeply into God's presence. People's hearts were prepared to receive it and many received edification and comfort through it.

At times we feel God is speaking a particular theme to us and we must discern what to do with it. Here are a few helpful questions for consideration:
- *Is what I sense compatible to the Word of God?* The prophetic word will not be contrary to God's written Word.
- *Is what I sense complimentary to what has already been spoken?* We prophesy in part (1 Cor. 13:9), but our part should not oppose what has already been spoken. Edification, not confusion, is our goal.
- *Is what I sense for the congregation or is it a personal word for me?* If it is personal, receive it. If it is corporate, communicate it.
- *Has it already been spoken?* If so, generally speaking, no reiteration is needed.
- *Is it the right time?* The Holy Spirit is eternal, knowing no time boundaries. Perhaps it is for a later time.

**Teaching the worship team to communicate**

Although the prophetic is generally considered spontaneous, I find that preparation is the key to flowing in the prophetic. Preparation doesn't hinder spontaneity, it gives the framework and discipline from which spontaneity can flow.

Did you ever stop and think of what some of the songs in the Bible might have sounded like? What did the celebration song of Exodus 15 sound like? How about the penitent psalm 51? What did the accompaniment to the words "As the deer pants for the streams of water, so my soul longs for you…" sound like. God has forever preserved the lyrics for us, but we will never know (this side of heaven) what the music sounded like. One thing is for sure, it probably was not anything like we might think it sounded. It was more "Eastern" sounding then "Western" sounding. It may not have even been very pleasant to our western ears, but it was to God. Despite the difference in culture and tonality, I believe that the victory songs had a victory sound. The intimate songs had an intimate sound. How do we learn to communicate sounds that are complimentary to the Word of the Lord that is coming forth?

Here are a few exercises I have incorporated with my teams over the years to try to help them communicate musically and grow in spontaneity:

**Exercise One**

Pick a song that has a particular theme: holiness, warfare/victory, intimacy, etc. Ask your band what they think that particular character trait *sounds* like. How can they reproduce that sound on their instrument?

When I teach group lessons with young worship musicians I assign them an emotion such as joy, anger, melancholy, etc. and give them one week to try to play that emotion on their instrument. The result is sometimes humorous, sometimes surprisingly moving. I want to teach them the difference between playing the notes and communicating the song. Sometimes I pick out a recording of a worship song for them which is uncommonly expressive and play it for them, asking their input afterwards. What made the song sound that way? What were the individual instruments doing in order to make the corporate sound? Classical music is also good for this.

In doing this exercise you find that certain chords, meters, chord progressions, and textures will create certain "feels". For example, if I walk up to a piano and play a diminished chord, there is a feeling of tension. If I play a Imaj7 chord followed by a IVmaj7 chord and repeat it, it will sound peaceful. The bVI, bVII, I progression has a majestic feel (see *"Possible Chord Progressions for Open Worship"*).

It is a good idea to start slowly and be consistent in working with your band on this. Pick out one or two songs in a set and just think about how to communicate them.

**Exercise Two**

The next step is to prepare to communicate as a band, spontaneously. In a service, if the Lord is exhorting us to step out and take the land, the sound from the band needs to be assertive, even aggressive, perhaps march-like and militant. Practice that sound in a practice session. Take your time and let it develop over 10 or 15 minutes. You will probably find that you run out of ideas and the freshness of the sound wears off quickly. When this happens, go back to the fundamental elements of music to discover how to expand your sound:

- Pitch – Pitches organized consecutively are called melody. Melody is only one element of musical expression, but it is one that is often left out of our "playing in the spirit." When an instrument plays a melody over the top of chords, another layer or texture is added.

    Pitches organized simultaneously are called harmony. When other instruments or voices add a harmony to a melody the plot thickens and expression multiplies.
- Rhythm – Timing and lengths of various sections can be altered. Don't just play two chords over and over again. Play those two chords for a time and then go into a different section with a different chord structure and then come back into the two chords. Varying Tempo (speed) and meter (time signatures) can produce diversity in the sounds you are making. Try different meters (three-four or six-eight time)
- Texture – This means different things happening at different times, hopefully complimenting each other. For example, most hymns are *homophonic*, meaning the soprano, alto tenor and bass parts all sing with the same rhythm. When the rhythms and shapes of the lines are dissimilar and independent, the texture is *polyphonic*. This contrast in texture makes the sound more interesting and effective.
- Intensity – this has to do with dynamic, or the "loudness" and "softness" of the sound. Remember that loud is only loud because of soft. If you start loud and stay loud, it will be boring. The same goes with soft. Vary the dynamic level of your music and you will not only be more expressive, but you will sound more mature as a band.
- Timbre – Timbre refers to the different tonal colors that come from various instruments and voices. If you put all colors together, you get brown. If all instruments play all the time you get an "brown" sound all the time. When the

instruments are in and out, or playing in pairs of sections (not on top of each other) a contrast of different tonal colors can be experienced.

**Exercise Three**

To incorporate the singers, assign a specific Psalm and have all of them open up their Bibles to that Psalm and get ready to sing. Explain to them that you will be playing a simple chord progression and that you want them to each take two or three verses of the Psalm and sing the exact words of the text to the music you play. Each will, of course, sing in his or her own style. As one finishes, the next one begins, continuing the thought with the next verses of the Psalm (You may want to break the ice by going first). This exercise helps the singers learn to flow together with one lyrical thought. It also gets them used to improvising a melody with a text that is already written.

**Exercise Four**

The next step with your singers is to give them a theme, not a Psalm, and have them expound that theme over a chord progression, as in the above exercise. This adds the dimension of improvising a lyric as well as a melody line. The words don't have to rhyme… they don't even have to have a great form. They do need to communicate the thought effectively. This is stepping out in a big way for some people. Some will naturally be better at it than others. Don't push it, but encourage them and they will grow in it.

These steps may help you. The Lord may give you other exercises that will be more effective in your context. The important thing here is that we are trying to move from an individual to a corporate expression of the prophetic. Of course, the more skillful you are on your instrument, the easier this process will be. You may want to look over the "*Spirit of Excellence – the role of skill in our worship*" section of this book.

Be sensitive to where the people you are leading are at in worship. Sometimes in our zeal to "take off" in the prophetic realm, we leave the congregation choking in our dust. They do not understand what we are doing and they can not follow. Be patient and let the Lord lead His flock!

# The Pastor/Worship Leader Relationship

Spiritual leaders and musicians can have wonderfully complimentary gifts. Together they can flow to create a powerful atmosphere for God to work in. Take Elisha and the musician, for example (2 Kings 3:15). When Elisha was called on to prophesy, he called for a musician. Their mutual giftings produced the Word of the Lord for the moment.

However, as is often the case, pastors and worship leaders can misunderstand each other and friction can result. Just as in a marriage, differences can be the cause of conflict or a source of strength in the relationship. I want to focus on how to recognize the reasons for misunderstandings and how to turn them into a strong relationship that is fruitful for the kingdom of God.

One obvious reason for misunderstandings between the two is a ***difference in vision.*** It can be very disappointing when the worship leader has a heart and a vision for worship and the pastor sees the "song service" as merely a time of getting people awake and prepared for the ministry of the Word (or vice versa). It can also be a disappointing when the pastor sees that worship is a dynamic experience with the presence of the living God that holds unlimited potential for effecting the congregation while the worship leader is focused on putting on a polished show.

Because our vision is a by-product of our values, we may be talking about a ***difference in philosophy*** here. We are driven by what we believe and when what we believe is different from those we are working with, confusion can result, making it very difficult and frustrating to work together.

*Communication and prayer are keys to resolving differences in vision.* Talk about your vision. Where there is no understood goal the worship tends to wander aimlessly. If one has a vision and the other does not, then pray for God to impart His vision (He is the only one who can do it) and to let His kingdom come and His will be done in your worship. Then watch Him answer. By the way, it is generally a great investment for a church to send the worship leader (or the worship team for that matter) to a good worship conference. Vision is really imparted when the team gets out of their "sphere" and experiences the unordinary.

If you are the worship leader and the pastor does not seem to have the same vision as you concerning worship, share your heart with him. Appeal to him humbly, remembering that he, as the pastor under Christ, is the final authority as to what happens in that local body. In 1 Chronicles 24, the musicians were under the authority of king David. Appeal to the Lord and then appeal to the pastor.

Another area of potential conflict is the ***difference in giftings***. Everybody is passionate for what they are gifted in. They think that their particular area of gifting is the most crucial to the health and well being of the body of Christ.

It is no different with pastors and worship leaders. The pastor/teacher might wonder why the worship leader wants to go on so long in the time of worship. The prophetic pastor might wonder why the worship leader does not just continue playing that one "anointed" song over and over every service. After all, it's working, why not wear it out? Of course the musician is the one who has to come up with those "anointed" songs. If he wears this one out in three weeks, then where does he find the next one? Some worship leaders are gifted administratively and it is difficult for them to flow spontaneously. Some are gifted prophetically and it is easy for them to "flow". However, the congregation doesn't always "flow" with them because what they do is over the head of the congregation. Sometimes it is just hard for a musician to go where you want him to. He is just not wired that way, at least not right now. But he can be discipled. It takes experience, training and maturity for a musician to be sensitive to the appropriateness of music and the direction of the Holy Spirit.

*Deference and bearing with one another are keys to resolving problems that result from differences of gifting.* Understanding that all the gifts are essential to the body, seeing a blind spot and making up for what lacks in another are important if we are to have a broad and accurate expression of Jesus within a congregation. We should not have a "us verses them" mentality. Work together in a mutual appreciation of each other's gifts and, again, *communicate*!

The next area is ***difference in personalities***. I am about as laid back as they come. Throughout my years in music ministry, God has seen fit to put me together with people who are, in many ways, diametrically opposed to my personality. The vision has not always been different, but the personalities have. I have to say that this has been one of the most difficult and most spiritually maturing things in my life. We have learned from each other and grown, but we have certainly rubbed each other wrong. *"As iron sharpens iron, so one man sharpens another."* (Proverbs 27:17) The sharpening process is not always easy, but sharp is always better then dull!

Many times a musician will have an "artistic" personality. Through the eyes of a left-brained pastor person, this translates into "strange, undisciplined, near-sighted, and sometimes seemingly apathetic." But don't forget, it was this "artistic person" in which you saw a gift that could be raised up.

Sometimes what we are talking about is a ***difference in maturity***. From time to time, for the simple reason that there is no one else to do the job, people get raised up prematurely. They may be good musicians, but they are spiritually immature. If that is the case, then we have to accept them where they are. But that is not where they have to stay!

*Understanding and discipleship are keys to resolving problems in personality and maturity.* Sometimes we musicians just need the pastor to pastor us, show us our blind spots and help us to mature in our personality and to understand his. Once again, a little communication can save a lot of heartache.

With a little maturity and a lot of communication these differences can be turned into strengths for the purposes of God in our churches.

*"I appeal to you, brothers, in the name of our Lord Jesus Christ, that all of you agree with one another so that there may be no divisions among you and that you may be perfectly united in mind and thought."*

1 Corinthians 1:10

# Worship and the Arts

There is no doubt that God desires to use the fine arts in this generation to glorify His Son and to bring people to salvation. The Bible tells us that all things were made for His pleasure (Rev. 4:11). We are also told to do what we do with all our hearts as unto the Lord (Col. 3:23). Those who are gifted in the arts are to use that gift to glorify God. Unfortunately, there has not been much of an outlet for them to do so in the church.

Do we give the world an opportunity to see the beauty of the Lord in our worship? Can they see His marvelous creativity in our worship? Psalm 27 exhorts us to behold the beauty of the Lord. The arts are a great way to see this beauty. Many things have been stolen by the world and consequently have been rejected by the church. It is true that these things done in the flesh can "rob" the glory from God. It is true that people can begin to "worship" what they create. Yet it is also true that God wants to restore these gifts and let His creativity flow back to Him in the beauty of expressive worship. This pleases Him.

This is not meant to be an exhaustive study on the use of the arts in worship. There are many excellent resources that can equip you much better in these areas than I could. This is simply to whet your appetite and to enlarge your vision for using different methods to worship God and to communicate the gospel.


**Banners**
Psalm 20:5 – *"In the name of our God we will set up banners."*

A banner is a piece of cloth attached to a staff, which is symbolic of a king or a kingdom. It is used as a signal. It is used to identify an allegiance. It can be used as a rallying point in battle. It rallies people for a common cause. It is a catalyst for involvement. It is used for celebration. It attracts attention. When used in worship it attracts attention to Jesus Christ and the attributes of God.

Banners were used historically in Israel. Because they were a part of the culture they knew what it meant to "lift up banners in His name." Numbers 2 tells us that the twelve tribes of Israel marched in the same order in which they camped, headed by their standards, or banners. Judah (which means praise) went first.

Moses gave the Lord the name "JEHOVAH-NISSI" (Exodus 17:15), which means "the Lord is my banner". In fact, Isaiah 11:1 says
*"Then it will come about in that day that the nations will resort to the root of Jesse, who will stand as the standard* (banner) *for the people; and his resting place will be glorious."*
JESUS IS GOD'S BANNER!

There is a theme in scripture of leading "captivity captive" and marching in "triumphant procession" (Judges 5:12; Ephesians 4:8; Colossians 2:15; Psalm 68:18). This is the idea of marching forth in triumphal procession with banners, declaring the victory of our Lord.

Banners are one way of making his praise glorious. We show the splendor of our God in splendid praise. I have to admit that there was a time that I was not crazy about banner worship. I thought of it as taking attention away from the Lord. No doubt, it can do that if not done in the right spirit. Yet, when done right, it truly glorifies Him. In recent years even denominational churches have begun reintroducing banners to worship.

Some churches have banner teams with elaborate choreographed presentations integrated into worship services. Some hang beautiful, colorful banners on the walls, reminding worshipers of some attribute of God as they worship. Others simply offer smaller, simpler flags for individuals to wave at will during worship services. There may be someone in your body with a tremendous gift of making banners that show forth the beauty and magnificence of our God. Encourage them in their gifting. It will edify the church.

**Dance**
Psalm 149:3 -- *"Let them praise His name with dancing..."*

Now here is one that the devil has definitely stolen away. The fact is that dancing is hardly ever mentioned in the Bible as merely a social amusement. It is most always associated with public or personal rejoicing and worship, both in Israel and in heathen nations. Dancing is the natural expression of joy. Many Psalms are "dance processions" which were recorded for us. They were an integral part of Old Testament worship. Many of the early New Testament church fathers, such as Chrysostom, Ambrose, Augustine and Gregory also confirm that dance was a part of the early church's form in worship.

One of the most powerful Bible pictures of dance in worship in 2 Samuel 6 when, with shear, passionate joy, and despite what others might think of him, David danced before the Lord with all his might. The sobering thought here is that Michal, David's wife, criticized, in fact, despised him, for this act of unhindered expression of praise. Verse 23 tells us that Michal was barren until the day of her death. Could it be that when genuine expressions of praise dance come forth, we might be in danger of being "barren" if we quench them?

The dance of David was spontaneous. The dance of the processions and other worship dances in ancient Israel seemed to have planned or choreographed. It follows then that both types of dancing are accepted and encouraged for our worship today. In fact, there are at least four kinds of dance we find in the scripture:

- Solo (David -- 2 Sam.6; Jephthah's daughter -- Judges 11:34)
- Company (Judges 21:21)
- Congregational (Miriam and the women -- Exodus 15)
- Declarative/Prophetic (1 Samuel 18:6)

Someone has said that when endeavoring to start a dance ministry it is good to "look before you leap". First, look to the Lord. Spend time in prayer for the right timing, the right people and direction. Second, look to the pastor and get his affirmation and vision for the ministry. Third, look to the Word and learn what it says about the ministry of dance. Fourth, look to seasoned ministry for guidance and insight. Lastly, look for the right people for the ministry.

If we are honest, we admit that in our times of worship we often run out of words to express our heart to the Lord. Perhaps if we set aside our cultural inhibitions and realize that dancing is "all right" with God, it would once again be "all right" with us and we would find a new release in worship that expresses our praise in ways our mere words can not.

**Drama**

Drama is a powerful and effective way to cut to the heart of people with the message of God. God used drama to communicate His message to His people through the prophets. What we see generally sticks in our minds much longer and moves us more than what we merely hear. I have known of dramatic productions that have brought literally thousands to Christ. I have been moved to greater consecration and service to the Lord after watching a moving drama.

The question might be raised "Is this actually worship?" While it is true that all drama is not necessarily worship, it can be a very effective agent in bringing people into worship. Why should the devil have all the good actors?

**Visual Art**

If all things were made by and for Jesus, why not turn all the artists in your congregation loose and let them make it a place of beauty, reflecting His resplendent beauty of the Lord? It is sad, but true that sometimes our meeting places are the drabbest, most uninspiring places. There are gifts in your body that can change that. Color, form, symmetry, texture, etc. all can greatly enhance the worship experience. Works of art can give concrete form to spiritual truths.

**God is the Divine Artist**

Beauty is a property of God and will always be so. Through art we can "behold the beauty of the Lord" (Psalm 27:4). We can all mentally agree that God wants to restore the arts to the church, where they rightfully belong. The question is are we giving Him a place to do that in our congregations? Do we create an atmosphere conducive to the full expression of the beauty of the Lord? Let's go before the Lord and seek Him as to what expression of His Son He would bring forth in our individual congregations.

# Appendix One
# Glossary of Musical Terms

**Accent** – To emphasize a note or chord

**Bar Line** – A vertical line that separates measures or bars

**Blues Scale** – A scale that is used in blues compositions; (1, b3, 4, #4, 5, b7) of a major scale

**Chord Progression** – the movement of one chord to another chord

**Chromatic Scale** – A scale consisting of all twelve half-step intervals of an octave

**Diatonic** - Notes found within a particular major scale

**Dominant** – The fifth degree of a major or minor scale. In functional harmony, a chord that comes before the tonic, or "home". For example: "C" is the tonic in the scale of C major. The dominant chord would be G.

**Dynamics** – Varying degrees of volume or intensity in a song

**Eighth note** – A note that is equal to one-half of a quarter note, or one half a beat

**Flat** – The symbol (b) that indicates to lower a pitch by one-half step; A pitch played or sung that is slightly lower than normal

**Form** – The organization and structure of a composition (song)

**Functional Harmony** – The part that a chord plays within a progression [Tonic (I), Subdominant (IV), Dominant (V)]

**Grand Staff** – The combination of the bass and treble staves

**Groove** – The "feel" of a song

**Half note** – A note equal to two quarter notes, or two beats

**Harmony** – Two or more tones sounded simultaneously

**Inversion** – A chord that has a note other than the root in the bass: a 1st inversion chord has a 3rd in the bass; a second inversion chord has the 5th in the bass.

**Key** – The tonal center of a composition

**Key signature** – A group of sharps or flats that appears at the beginning of a staff which indicate the key

**Legato** – To play smoothly and connected

**Major Scale** – A scale made up of a certain pattern of intervals, or steps (Whole, Whole, Half, Whole, Whole, Whole Half)

**Measure** – The notes and rests between two bar lines

**Medley** - An arrangement that links together two or more songs

**Melody** – A succession of single notes

**Minor Scale** –
    Natural Minor 1,2,b3,4,5,b6,b7
    Harmonic Minor 1,2,b3,4,5,b6,7

**Mode** – A group of notes arranged into a specific scale

**Natural** – The symbol that indicates that a note is neither sharp nor flat

**Pentatonic Scale** – A five note scale used much in modern music (1,2,3,5,6) of a major scale

**Pitch** – The location of a note related to it's highness or lowness

**Poly Chord** – A single chord created by combining two or more chords

**Quarter note** – A note that has a rhythmic value of one beat

**Relative minor** – A minor key that has the same key signature as it's related major key (C and A minor have the same key signatures, as do G and E minor

**Rest** – A period of silence; the symbols used to indicate a silence

**Rhythm** – The pattern or flow of beat in a song; the duration of pitches in a melody or accompaniment.

**Seventh chords** – A chord consisting of a root, a third, a seventh , and sometimes a fifth

**Sharp** – The symbol (#) that indicates to raise the pitch one-half step; A pitch played or sung that is slightly higher than normal

**Sixteenth note** – A note one half the length of an eighth note, or one-fourth a beat

**Slur** – A curved line notated above or below two or more lines that indicates that they are to be played legato

**Staccato** – To play short and detached

**Staff** – The horizontal lines on or in between which notes are written

**Subdominant** – The fourth degree of a major or minor scale. In functional harmony, the chord that comes before a dominant chord.

**Syncopation** – To shift the accent of a note or chord to a weak beat or the weak part of a beat.

**Tempo** – The speed of a song or section

**Tie** – A curved line that joins two notes of the same pitch that lasts the duration of both values

**Time signature** – A sign placed after the clef and the key signature at the beginning of a piece that indicates the meter of the piece

**Tonic** – The first note of a scale or key. The "home" chord in a chord progression.

**Transpose** – To change a composition from one key to another

**Triad** – A three note chord usually consisting of a root, a third and a fifth

**Voicing** – How notes are arranged in a chord

**Whole note** – A note equal to the length of two half notes, or four beats

# Appendix Two
# Modes of the Major Scale

A MODE is a group of notes arranged into a specific scale. From these scales we derive different harmony groups. It is easy to understand different modes by comparing them to their parallel major scales. Below are the modes of the major scale. Each mode begins on a different degree of the scale. Note that each mode stays true to the key of it's original major scale, although it starts on a different note. For example, D dorian is simply a C major scale played from D to D; G mixolydian is a C major scale played from G to G, etc.

A knowledge of the modes is helpful in understanding improvisation. For example, one can improvise over an A minor key (aeolian mode) by using the notes in a C major scale. All of the notes will sound good but some will sound better than others.

To get your feet wet playing modes, take a song in the key of E minor and practice improvising the E aeolian scale over it. You can think "G major" since E aeolian is a mode of the G major scale, but you will find that if you center around the G note it will not sound right. That's because the key center is E (you are in the key of E minor). You can also an E dorian scale, the only difference being the raised 6th scale degree (C#).

C Major (Ionian)

D Dorian (b3, b7)

E Phrygian (b2, b3, b6, b7)

F Lydian (#4)

G Mixolydian (b7)

A Aeolian (b3, b6, b7)

B Locrean (b2, b3, b5, b6, b7)

# Appendix Three
# Guitar Chord Library

Below are guitar fingerings for some of the most common chords in the most commonly played keys. Chords in the keys that are not shown can be fingered by using the barre chords in the key directly above or below the desired key and moving them to the correct fret or by capoing up or down. Chord books are available that show chords and inversions in all keys. These are a great tool for helping you to get to know your fretboard.

# Guitar Chord Library (continued)

www.ingramcontent.com/pod-product-compliance
Lightning Source LLC
Chambersburg PA
CBHW080547170426
43195CB00016B/2703